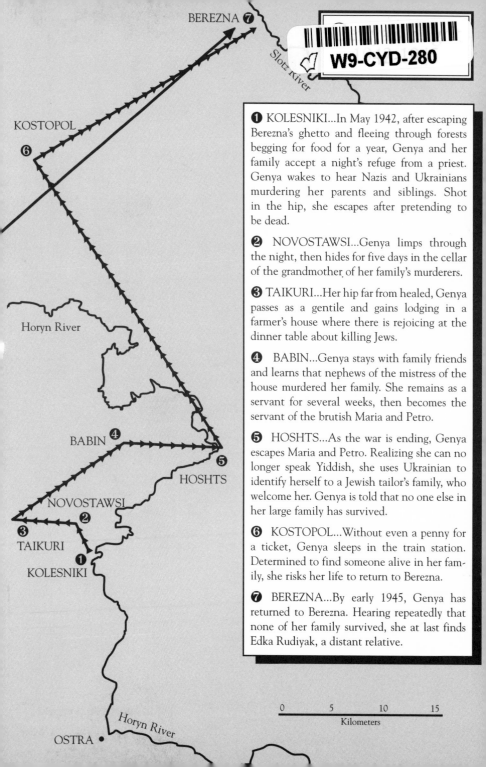

BEREZNA ❼

Slotz River

W9-CYD-280

KOSTOPOL
❻

Horyn River

BABIN ❹

❺
HOSHTS

NOVOSTAWSI
❷

❸
TAIKURI
❶
KOLESNIKI

Horyn River

OSTRA •

| 0 | 5 | 10 | 15 |

Kilometers

❶ KOLESNIKI...In May 1942, after escaping Berezna's ghetto and fleeing through forests begging for food for a year, Genya and her family accept a night's refuge from a priest. Genya wakes to hear Nazis and Ukrainians murdering her parents and siblings. Shot in the hip, she escapes after pretending to be dead.

❷ NOVOSTAWSI...Genya limps through the night, then hides for five days in the cellar of the grandmother of her family's murderers.

❸ TAIKURI...Her hip far from healed, Genya passes as a gentile and gains lodging in a farmer's house where there is rejoicing at the dinner table about killing Jews.

❹ BABIN...Genya stays with family friends and learns that nephews of the mistress of the house murdered her family. She remains as a servant for several weeks, then becomes the servant of the brutish Maria and Petro.

❺ HOSHTS...As the war is ending, Genya escapes Maria and Petro. Realizing she can no longer speak Yiddish, she uses Ukrainian to identify herself to a Jewish tailor's family, who welcome her. Genya is told that no one else in her large family has survived.

❻ KOSTOPOL...Without even a penny for a ticket, Genya sleeps in the train station. Determined to find someone alive in her family, she risks her life to return to Berezna.

❼ BEREZNA...By early 1945, Genya has returned to Berezna. Hearing repeatedly that none of her family survived, she at last finds Edka Rudiyak, a distant relative.

GENYA

Left on her own

at the age of eleven,

she survived

the Holocaust

GENYA

BY GENYA FINKELSTEIN

Translated from the Hebrew by Shuli Sharvit

GT
PUBLISHING

THIS BOOK IS DEDICATED TO THE MEMORY OF
MY PARENTS, RAIZEL AND WOLF FINKELSTEIN;
MY BROTHERS, YOSSELE, SHAYE AND LEIBELE;
AND TO THE REST OF MY BULBA AND FINKELSTEIN
RELATIVES WHO PERISHED IN THE HOLOCAUST.
I LOVE YOU AND MISS YOU SO MUCH. . . .

CONTENTS

ACKNOWLEDGMENTS

With deepest gratitude to my loved ones.

To my husband, Eli, for his love and patience throughout the entire process.

To my son, Didi, for his assistance in publishing the book.

To my grandchildren, Efrat and Oren, for their constant support and their contribution to parts of the book.

And special thanks to my daughter, Vered, who devoted time, patience and so much love so that this book could be published.

THIS BOOK IS ALSO A MEMORIAL TO MY FIRST HUSBAND,

MORDECHAI (MOTTI) TUVI (SCHWARTZ),

WHO DIED IN ISRAEL IN 1964;

TO HIS PARENTS, TOVAH AND PERETZ SCHWARTZ;

AND TO HIS SISTERS AND BROTHER, CHAYA,

DEVORAH AND MOSHE,

ALL OF WHOM PERISHED IN THE HOLOCAUST.

A special word of thanks to Mr. Walter H. Weiner—a wonderful man, without whose sensitive support, understanding and invaluable assistance the production and translation of this book would not have been possible: *"May you go from strength to strength."*

This book carries two weighty messages, the first in the form of a question: How would the reader have turned out if he or she had endured what Genya went through between eleven and fourteen years of age? Assume you (the reader) are not quite eleven years old and hiding in a deep puddle of muck while hearing your mother plead for mercy for your three brothers and your adopted sister. The pleading is to no avail and both of your parents and all of your siblings are killed. Then a bullet hits you in the hip as you try to run away.

What kind of adult would you have become after this experience and the many other horrors that Genya describes, including the incredible death of her first husband who gave her the only love she knew after years of unbelievable misery? Would you now (more than fifty years later) be a misanthropic, half-crazed, non-communicative, non-productive outcast of society, totally and bitterly absorbed by your nightmares and your constant physical pain? Or would you, like Genya, be a productive, giving, 67-year-old mother, grandmother, and wife who spends her time collecting clothing and food for the poor, and in other ways helping those "less fortunate" than she?

Either way you would certainly want the world to remember what you and millions like you suffered at the hands of the Nazi butchers and the Ukrainians who worked with them. You would want to keep your promise to your long-gone family that they would never be forgotten.

That is the second message—the world must never forget! Not Genya's generation, which still can conjure up fresh memories of the Holocaust, nor younger generations, which must rely on reading works like this book, written by survivors, and listening to those who can remember seeing the atrocities uncovered as the death camps were liberated. It is the duty of all people, Jews and non-Jews, to help preserve the experiences of those who suffered those horrors so that their experiences will be remembered forever. Every reader of this book owes it to his and her progeny to learn about Genya and think, "But for the grace of God, I could have been Genya."

Why am I, almost a second-generation American, writing this foreword? The answer lies in the word "almost." My mother was born in the United States and lived here all her life. My father lived in the United States since he was five years old. But my father, both of his parents, and, so far as I know, all of his grandparents were born in Berezna—the same shtetl, in what is now Ukraine, from which Genya came.

So, with my Berezna connection*, and being only four

---

*Another motive for my desire to have this book published is to feed my interest in information about Berezna, its people and its history. If any reader also has a Berezna connection or knows people who have information about Berezna or people who have origins in Berezna, I would like to hear from you or them. Communications should be addressed to Walter Weiner, 452 Fifth Avenue, New York, NY 10018.

months older than Genya, I thought to myself many times while and after reading this book, "But for the grace of God...". Almost all of my father's family, on both his mother's and his father's sides, emigrated to the United States before World War I. But there again is the word "almost." My grandmother's older sister, Czerna, stayed in Berezna with a daughter and, ultimately, grandchildren. Czerna's son, Sam, did emigrate to the U.S. in the early 1900's, and Sam's son and daughter are my favorite cousins. Did Czerna, who was my great-aunt, and her family suffer the same fate as Genya's family or were they "merely" machine-gunned into a mass grave and sprinkled with quick lime?

I discovered Genya and the Hebrew version of this book in September 1996, after having informed a number of individuals and organizations in Israel (including Margalit Schlain of Yad Vashem in Ramat Gan) of my interest in the shtetl called Berezna. When I heard some of the events described in this book through the patient efforts of my wife, Nina, who is fluent in Hebrew, and then learned more about Genya as a person, I decided that an English version of this book must be published.

While many people have helped with this book in many ways, and are acknowledged by Genya, I want to make special mention of three men who epitomize what it means to be "good Jews." Being of Syrian Sephardic origin, they have little or no experience or background with Eastern European shtetls. However, Joe, Stanley, and Ken Cayre believe strongly that the Holocaust was a Jewish experience, not just an Ashkenazic experience, and they want Genya's story to reach as many people as possible. They want this story to bring tears to the eyes of all readers, just as it has to theirs. The world owes a debt of gratitude to the brothers Cayre for donating the services of their company, Good Times Publishing, and making this book possible.

I am particularly grateful to the Cayres because someday I want my three-year-old grandson, Josh, to read *Genya* and to think about his great-grandfather, who he will never remember (my father died July 13, 1997), playing in the mud and dust of Berezna just as Genya did (but in the much poorer end of town). I want Josh to think, what if his great-great-grandparents hadn't been brave enough to take that frightening trip to New York in steerage ninety years ago? I also want him to think about how terrible, unthinkable experiences can produce a giant of a person, like Genya, if that person has the fortitude and determination to live through the worst kinds of hardships and still believe, like Genya, that people can be good.

Finally, I want the reader to know that at one moment the author suggested entitling her book *Only Heaven Cried*. It sounded like a good idea at first. But then we decided: "No, Genya! Not only Heaven cried. We all cried, and we will continue to cry as long as a single copy of your book exists."

WALTER H. WEINER
MAY 1998

PREFACE

Decades of a peaceful life in a tranquil neighborhood have not erased the horrors.

A comfortable home, a yard filled with flowers, a loving family, all these have not succeeded in warding off the dreams at night and the terrors in the day.

Last night I had a dream. In my dream I saw Father and Mother. Their faces were very distinct. My small brothers, Yossele, Shayele and Leibele, also appeared in the dream, but I didn't remember their faces. I so wanted the dream to go on and on. I so wanted not to part from them.

Mother was so lovely in the dream. She was dressed in a fancy pink silk dress; on her head was a felt hat with a net veil that concealed her eyes; and a delicate pearl chain hung around her neck.

In my dream we are in Kremnitz, a spectacular resort town where we vacationed frequently when I was a small girl. I saw so clearly the palace that stood at the top of the hill, a magnificently beautiful palace. I saw the waterfalls and profusion of plants and multicolored flowers, whose delicate fragrance wafted all around.

Yesterday, in my dream, once again I saw Grandfather Finkelstein, and he was lying in a puddle of mud. He was all blood-soaked, struggling with his last vestiges of strength to extricate himself from the puddle. I extended a hand to him, trying to help him. No. I lacked the strength to rescue Grandfather Noah from the pit.

I awoke drenched in sweat and seized with dread.

Hadn't I pledged that if I were to remain alive I would write and tell the story?

I want today's youth to read, to know and never to forget.

one

Childhood in Berezna

I was born in the village of Berezna in Ukraine on December 15, 1930. I was the eldest daughter of Raizel Bulba and Wolf Finkelstein.

The village of Berezna derived its name from the white-barked berozah tree and was situated in an area of swamps, forests and marshlands, dotted with country homes. Here and there a farmer would plow his land, his horse harnessed to the plow. Violet and white lilac trees bloomed there in profusion, emitting their intoxicating fragrance. Every time I see a lilac or inhale its scent, I return to the blissful days of my childhood.

The majority of Berezna's residents were Jews, with a minority of Provoslavians and Catholic Poles who had settled there after its conquest by Poland in 1920. As in the majority of villages in Volynhia, the Jews of Berezna dealt in fabrics, leathers and lumber. And there were also tailors and shoemakers among them, teachers and butchers, wagoners and tinkers.

Three children were born to my parents after me— Yossele, who was six years younger than I; Shaye, who was born two years after him; and the last, Leibele, who was born in 1940, in the midst of war.

Our house was made of red brick with a wooden-shingled roof. Nearby lived Uncle Itzik, my mother's brother, and my mother's grandfather and grandmother, Chaim and Esther Bulba. The three homes stood in a great courtyard, not far from the church on Koschelna Street. In the rear of the courtyard stood the family's soft drink factory. Most of the yard was covered with sand and weeds, and in the winter the sand was transformed into a giant mud puddle. The streets were perpetually muddy, and split logs were laid across the width of the road to help pedestrians cross. Only the main roads, such as Komisarska Street, were paved with cobblestones.

I remember the windows of the houses, adorned with flowering plants and double glazed with wooden gratings placed between the layers of glass in the winter to keep the heat inside and provide a barrier against the fierce cold. Between the glazes people would also place rosy-cheeked apples for storage during the winter months. These were beautiful to see, the low winter sun slanting through windows full of blushing fruit. Before Passover, with the start of spring, they would take apart the double glazing, and we, the children, were favored with the sweet apples. Thus began the era of my childhood, amidst an abundance of love and beauty.

When I was about nine, my parents adopted seventeen-year-old Rivkah. She was a motherless orphan from a large family. At first she came to spend the summer vacation with us and to help my mother care for my small brothers.

She became very close to us, especially to my mother, and she asked to stay and live with us. At times I was jealous of Rivkahle. "Why does she have more dresses than I?" I would ask my mother contrarily. And she, good soul, would explain to me that Rivkahle was a bigger girl and had different needs. "When you are her age," she would say to me, "you will have the same things, if not more."

Until the age of six I was an only child. I remember when I realized that my mother's stomach was expanding. I asked her for an explanation, and Mother replied that the stork had brought us a baby and that when he was big enough, he would be born, and I would have a little brother or sister to play with. One morning my parents woke me up. It was cold outside, and they dressed me in warm clothing. Father told me that we were going to the home of our relatives, Pessya and Yankel (Yankel was my father's brother) and their daughter, Manya, because Mother didn't feel well and required peace and quiet. I was dismayed. I loved being at home, and I certainly didn't want to leave when clearly something secret and totally foreign to me was going to take place. But there was no way I could change my father's plan.

After several days Father came to take me home. On the way he told me that we had a new little baby and his name was Yossele. At home a myriad of preparations were underway. The aunts and uncles came to visit and offer their assistance. They were all so busy that no one had time to say hello to me. Domka, our gentile maid, was busy boiling water with chamomile petals in which to bathe the infant. She strained the water through a washcloth into an oaken tub that the neighboring farmers had built. After the water cooled off a bit, she bathed my little brother in it. Yossele had delicate pink skin, and he was covered with a fine down.

Mother sat in bed watching, overcome with emotion as they bathed the tender newborn. Domka dried him and wrapped him expertly in a large white diaper. Afterwards she dressed him in a wool angora outfit that Aunt Gessya had knitted and tucked him in beside Mother. The baby looked beautiful to me, and I wondered why they wrapped his legs in cotton gauze. "So that he should grow straight," they told me.

Mother took the baby to her bosom and nursed him. I stood by filled with wonder and emotion. I felt so grown-up. I was the big one and had a little brother. "You will be his friend," said Mother with a smile, kissing me on the cheek. I ran outside joyfully, and I told my friends who had gathered at our door that we had a new baby boy named Yossele. I told them that in a week, they would make a *brith* (the ceremony of the circumcision) for him. My Polish friends did not know what a *brith* was, and I didn't know how to explain it to them, but I knew enough to tell them that there would be a big celebration at our house.

Everyone came to Yossele's *brith*. No one from our extended family was absent. My mother's grandfather and grandmother, who were then over eighty years old, came with their widowed daughter, Rudya, who lived with them. She was very fat. Today I would guess that she weighed two hundred and fifty pounds!

Everyone's attention focused on the Nissingoltz couple. Aunt Sheindel Nissingoltz, Father's older sister, was wealthy and extremely well groomed. Her husband, Levi Nissingoltz, a tall, handsome man with a slight paunch, was a big contractor in Ostra and the surrounding area. He amassed his wealth building barracks for the soldiers of the Polish Army. He was always handsomely dressed and wore an exquisitely tailored suit.

It was a boisterous and jolly group, scattered throughout the Volynhia region. Aunt Gittel, Aunt Bayla, Aunt Gessya, Uncle Yankel, Aunt Pessya and other relatives arrived. From far and near they all came to share in our joy, dressed in their best finery. Only our relatives from Father's side who lived in Slavuta and Shpatovka in Russia were unable to come, because it was not possible to cross the Russian-Polish border.

Everyone who came to the *brith* brought delicacies, but the jewel in the crown was the gefilte fish (stuffed fish) tasting of the Garden of Eden, which Mother herself had prepared despite her weakness. No other woman in the family could prepare gefilte fish as tasty as Mother's. The fresh fish were brought from the Slotz River, which flowed only a little over a mile from our home. Domka cleaned them and filleted them with a big knife, a type of metal ax we called a *hak meser* (chopping knife). I loved watching Mother while she worked in the kitchen. I remember Mother explaining to me that we must always remove the fish's tail, scales and eyes in order to prevent bitterness. I was a curious child, and I loved learning kitchen secrets from her. I inherited her love of cooking, and even today when I cook, I am reminded of her delicacies and the way in which she would prepare them.

Grandfather Noah Finkelstein, Father's father, was the godfather (*Zandek*) of the *brith* and held the baby in his arms during the actual circumcision. The rejoicing was seven-fold because, indeed, Yossele was the first boy in our family. Everyone drank *"L'chaim*, To Life!" from the bottles of vodka and vishniac that Father had prepared, and devoured Mother's wonderful stuffed fish, apple cakes and poppy-seed pastries.

The aunts also brought me many beautiful presents. But the main attraction was the small infant. And I, who had always been the center of attention, was suddenly thrust aside. Father, however, realized what was happening and showered me with affection.

Uncle Itzik, Mother's brother, brought me a box of chocolates. He knew that I collected the colorful gold wrappers in order to trade them with my friends. I loved Uncle Itzik very much. He had a special way of relating to children, even though he himself did not have any. He put me on his knee and whispered that the baby was not any-where near as beautiful as I was. When I was promoted to first grade, he bought me a navy coat and beret, the most beautiful in Berezna. That is what Uncle Itzik was like.

—

two

Household Smells

In the kitchen of our home there was a wooden wall. Brass pots and pans, passed down through generations, were hung from hooks and pegs on that wall. Mother was very strict about Domka polishing and shining them with cleansers and sand. They used those pots to cook jams in the summer from the seasonal fruits—plums, cherries and wild berries. I remember Mother standing outside, stirring the big pots.

Even Mother's preparation of noodles was conducted with great care, like a sacred ritual. With her hands, she would knead the dough made of eggs and flour, rolling it on the *lokshen breitel*, the board used to cut the noodles, and then spreading it to dry on a white tablecloth. Afterwards she would fold the dough and quickly roll and cut it into thin strands, which she would dry out once again. Those noodles were wonderful.

It seems to me that we were not very wealthy, but a sense of plenty was always present in our home. Nothing was ever lacking, not food and not clothing, and the house was always filled with the pleasant smells of cooking. On

Friday they would slaughter the chickens for the Sabbath and purchase a lot of high-quality, flavorful beef. The maid would pluck the chicken feathers and kosher the chickens with coarse salt. Friday morning at dawn we would bake the braided loaves, the challahs, and cakes for the Sabbath, and all day the odors of a bakery, fresh and fragrant, would spread through the house. Grandmother would prepare *pletzels*, a type of flat bread with minced onions, for everyone, as well as other types, sprinkled with lots of poppy seeds. We ate the *pletzels* with delicious fresh sour cream or with butter. On the Sabbath Domka would bring wood and coal to heat the house and to stoke the large furnace. And Sunday was her day off.

Father and Mother met in the city of Rovna. Mother was born in Berezna. Her parents were Golda and Noah Bulba. Golda was born in the village of Lotsk, near the city of Rovna, and she passed away when my mother was twelve years old. Golda had five sisters. Grandfather Noah was left a young widower, caring for five children, two sons and three daughters. Several years later he married Rachel, a devoutly religious woman from Lithuania.

Father was born in the city of Ostra, near the Polish-Russian border close to the Horyn River. Father's father was also called Noah, Noah Finkelstein, and he too was widowed when Father was a young boy. He also remarried. His second wife was named Esther. This Esther was a grandmother to me in every sense. Father had three sisters: Bayla, who lived in Rovna and had a fruit store, and

Sheindel and Gittel, who lived in Ostra, the city where father and his sisters were born.

Mother came to Rovna to pursue her studies, and apparently she met Father in Bayla's fruit store. Once a "delegation" of father's friends arrived at Mother's home to see how a motherless household was run, and they were pleasantly surprised by her immaculate home—it was neat as a pin and absolutely spotless. Mother, who was a young girl at the time, made a special impression with her wonderful cooking. The engagement was arranged with lots of rejoicing, and when Mother finished her studies at the gymnasium, the couple were wed. Uncle Moshe, Mother's oldest brother, told me all this. Uncle Moshe had been a Zionist pioneer in his youth, but he later settled in Argentina with his wife, Leah, who had relatives there.

Father and Mother shared a truly extraordinary love for each other. Father always used to hug Mother and kiss her, and she would respond with great tenderness. Father was a tall, well-built man, very particular about his appearance and clothes. He had a handsome nose, and the gentiles used to say that his nose did not look "Jewish." I inherited his dark eyes. When I was born they named me Golda, after my mother's dead mother, but since I attended a Polish school and mingled with Polish and Ukrainian children, my parents decided to exchange my Jewish name, Golda, for the Polish name Genya.

I was an excellent student. The teacher adored me. She praised me constantly for my beautiful penmanship and correct answers. She was a Polish gentile who had arrived in our village from Krakow in Galicia when she married a

Polish doctor from Berezna. The Polish and Ukrainian children in the class did not like the praise I received from the teacher, and more than once they showed it by hitting me. "They are jealous of you," Mother would say. The gentile children also made my Jewish friend Ruchele's life miserable. Her facial features were extremely "Jewish," and the children made fun of her "Jewish" nose. They also tormented my non-Jewish friend Stefa for being friendly with Jews. More than once Ruchele and I found hateful and poisonous notes in our schoolbags bearing anti-Semitic slurs such as *Jidka, itcha du Paleshtina* (Jews, get out and go to Palestine. You are not needed here). Occasionally they accused us of murdering Jesus and of using gentile children's blood for baking matzoth. And once the gentiles in my class even placed a frog in my lunch bag. Only many years later did I realize the full meaning and consequences of these "childish" pranks.

We grew up in the comfortable, rural environment of a small village. We were high-spirited Jewish kids, and we played plenty of pranks. My friends started rumors about white-robed figures floating about in the night in the vicinity of the Polish priest's home, in the courtyard of the church. We decided to investigate the matter. One of the older youths, Shloimele, freckled and bold, climbed atop the church fence in order to observe the demons and spirits in the priest's yard. The noise woke the priest and he went outside to the churchyard in his long, white night clothes and frightened Shloimele half to death. The priest locked Shloimele in the church, called the police and told his parents what their son had done.

Another time, we were playing hide and seek among the gas canisters used for manufacturing soft drinks in the family soda factory. Entrance to the plant was strictly forbidden, but nevertheless we would play there whenever we felt like it, and no one was any the wiser until once one of the canisters exploded, followed by several smaller containers. One of the female workers, a bottle washer, was slightly injured on her neck and face. We were all frightened out of our wits. My cousin Chavale, an older girl and a true leader but the most mischievous in the group, convinced us that it was best not to return home. "Uncle Itzik will probably be very angry," she said, "and he will surely beat us." We ran from the soda factory and hid in the old city district. When evening came and we had not returned home, the family members started looking for us. One relative, a woman named Bolka Barder, found us. She convinced us to return home and promised that nothing terrible would happen. And, indeed, that is what occurred. Uncle Itzik good-naturedly explained to us that sometimes mischievous pranks end badly, and that we were very lucky that more serious damage had not been done.

Grandfather Noah Bulba was a fine man with a great zest for life. He was fair-haired with a light brown, well-groomed beard and large green, laughing eyes. In the mornings he would knock on our door and wake us, both hands filled with fresh treats from the market—one with fruits and the other with butter, cream or chocolate. He never arrived at our door empty-handed.

I remember him returning home on Friday nights after praying in the synagogue. He was dressed in his Sabbath clothes and always hummed a tune. Grandfather Noah Bulba and his wife, Rachel, lived not far from us, and on Friday nights we would sometimes join them for the Sabbath meal. The table was always set very festively and decorated with shining silver candlesticks and gleaming silverware. Step-grandmother Rachel was very strict about observing religious laws and customs, much more than was traditional in our family, and I viewed her as a harsh woman. Nevertheless, I loved sleeping in the big wooden bed in their house after the Sabbath meal. It was from Rachel that I learned the morning prayer *Modeh Ani Lefanecha* (I give thanks before You). It was she who taught me that on the Sabbath it was forbidden to comb one's hair, that one should only pat it into place, and that it was very important to be vigilant and never mix, G-d forbid, meat and dairy dishes.

Father always worked very hard. He and his brother, Uncle Yankel Finkelstein, traded in fruit. They would purchase the fruit—apples, pears and cherries—wholesale from the orchard for marketing and exporting. There were prosperous years and lean ones, depending on the weather the previous winter. They would also ship the fruit to far-away places, even sending it to the capital city of Warsaw. I loved waiting for Father to return from his travels. He would always bring us treats we adored. I remember the halavah he would buy in Warsaw, covered in foil wrapping paper decorated with red stripes.

One day Father and Uncle Yankel were late returning home from their trip to Warsaw. Mother was very worried. We knew they traveled from Warsaw by train and that from the station they would hire a wagon with a pair of horses and a driver. When they arrived late that night, we learned that Ukrainian bandits had attacked them on the road and robbed them of all their money. They were both beaten and bruised. Blood was dripping from Uncle Yankel's nose, and Mother hurried to apply ice cubes to stanch the flow.

In the summer we would travel to a *dacha* (a small summer home) across the Slotz River, which divided Berezna in two. There were forests of pine trees there and small, charming country log cabins, which the Poles would rent to the Jews for the summer months. All of us went: Mother and the children; Aunt Chayka, mother's older sister, and her children; and our beautiful unmarried aunt, Gessya. Father and the uncles would join us on the weekends. Domka would remain at home and join us on the weekends to help Mother prepare the delicious Sabbath dishes. On the Sabbaths when she did not come, we ate cold meals because there was no one to warm up the food. We spent the summer days in peace and quiet; we sailed across the river, hiked in the pine forests, caught butterflies, inhaled the pure air and bought tasty fresh food from the local villagers—chickens, fruit and butter. Mother would always say that the children gained weight and healthy color in their cheeks during these vacations.

Father and Mother would not permit us to bathe in the river unless we were accompanied by adults. They would tell us about the Gentile girls who would go bathing in the river and drown because they did not know how to swim. More than once we observed a body being pulled from the river. The grandfathers would go into the water wearing their *gatkes* (long white cotton underpants) and the young folk, male and female, would wear modest swimming suits.

I remember peeling oranges from the land of Israel, stamped with the word "Jaffa." Mother would carefully save these peels, dry them out in the oven and then crush them to use in her wonderful cakes.

I loved Mother's food. Father always said that no other woman he knew—not his sisters and not mother's sisters—could cook as well as she did. Goose fat, for instance. I will never forget the special steps she used to prepare goose fat. It would be prepared in winter so that it would be ready for Passover. Even prior to Chanukah she would buy about twenty geese, which were ritually slaughtered by the *shochet* (slaughterer), and another maid in addition to Domka would come from the village. Even Father would participate in the project. After their feathers were plucked, the geese would be hung over a burning flame to remove the last tiny feathers. Afterwards they would be split and cleaned. The next stage involved separating the meat from the fat. We would store the meat in the cellar and prepare roasts and soups over the course of the next several weeks. The last step would be frying the fat with minced onions and storing it in earthenware pots in the cellar.

Mother was known through the entire village for her great beauty. She was of average height with fair hair and skin and green eyes, and she was full of energy, her actions very quick. Uncle Moshe used to say that she was the most fastidious person he knew when it came to cleanliness and order. After the maid would scrub the wooden floors of our home and rub them with wax, Mother would not let anyone walk on them for a full hour. She would notice immediately if anyone moved a towel in the linen closet. Mother also loved to help, and she helped everyone.

Uncle Itzik lived in Grandmother Esther's house and was the chief manager of the soft drink factory. The "citronada" and raspberry punches made at our family plant were in demand throughout the entire region. The factory was full to overflowing with red, green and yellow bottles, as well as seltzer siphons. The plant always gleamed and sparkled. Everything was produced naturally, without artificial colors or chemicals. Farmers from the surrounding countryside would bring us their fruits: wild strawberries, raspberries, blackberries and more. The fruits would cook for a long time in a giant pot, and their sweet, fruity smells spread through the entire building.

In the winter months, blocks of ice would be brought from the river by wagon to be stored in a giant pit in the factory's yard. In the summer they would be used to cool the drinks, and shopkeepers from the area would come to buy large amounts of the drinks and the blocks of ice.

I also remember the washday rituals. This job was given to a different maid, because Domka was always busy with other work. The *pratska* ("washerwoman" in Ukrainian) would come for the washing, a project that always lasted a minimum of two days. During the month all the sheets, bedding, towels and clothing were stored; the washerwoman would scrub them on a wooden washboard with a mound of soap and powdered detergent that was called Radion. Even today I can still see before my eyes the advertisements posted at the entrance of the local groceries and clothing stores: *Radion sam-piaja*, meaning, "Radion cleans by itself."

They would boil water in a great tin kettle in the yard, over a bonfire of wood and coal. Afterwards the sheets and towels smelled wonderfully fresh because of the starch and the blue liquid detergents that they added to the water. The wash was hung to dry on clotheslines in our large yard, while Domka smoothed the sheets and tablecloths with a wooden roller. The other clothes were pressed with a coal-heated iron. We were always beautifully dressed and immaculately turned out. Worn-out clothing was packed in bundles and sent to needy Jews and to orphanages.

I still remember what we used to do in Berezna to ward off the flies on summer days. We would hang paper strips smeared with glue from the ceiling, and the flies would stick to them. When the strips were covered with the tiny corpses, we would change them for fresh ones. The discovery of flypaper was viewed then as one of the greatest inventions of its time. I also remember the village black-smith, a man of huge girth who was one hundred years old when he died. The elderly Grandmother Esther brought word of his death. She entered the house and spit, *Tfu, tfu, nisht da gedacht* (It should not happen here). And I remember the cramped houses clustered around the main square and Leizer, the *shochet*, dressed in his long coat and with his neatly trimmed beard, passing by the stores and businesses an hour or so before candle-lighting on Friday evenings, calling out loudly, *"Shabos, Shabos! Noah, farmach! Man darf gayen in bod"* (Sabbath, Sabbath! Noah, lock up! It is time for the ritual bath!). And Grandfather Noah would urge my Aunt Gessya to close her notions shop, from which all the village tailors purchased zippers, thread and buttons, and he would rush home to greet the Sabbath.

Domka learned all the customs of a Jewish home. She knew the difference between meat and dairy dishes and how to kosher meat. She would prepare *cholent* for the Sabbath exactly as Mother had taught her. They would place the *cholent* in the oven for the entire night, and it would bubble in the pot until noon on Saturday. Mother would also bake a *kugel*, a sweet noodle pudding, for the Sabbath. We would begin the noontime Sabbath meal with a radish salad: Domka grated white radishes, added minced onions, a hard-boiled egg and goose fat and mixed it all together. A true delicacy! When everything was ready, Domka would announce in a loud voice, "Mistress Raizel! The food is ready! The table is set! Where is the master of the house?"

Father would return home from the synagogue every Saturday at noon. He would perform the ritual hand-washing and join us at the table. Mother, my little brothers, my adopted sister Rivkah and I would already be waiting for him there. Woe to any latecomer! Father was very strict in these matters. He also demanded behavior appropriate to the dinner table. One day a discussion concerning synagogue affairs came up, and in the heat of the discussion, Grandfather Noah Finkelstein's false teeth fell on the floor! My brother Yossele and I exploded with laughter. We were sent away from the table in disgrace. Eventually Mother took pity on us, and after two hours called us down to eat.

On Sundays during the summer vacation, I would go with Rivkah to pick sorrel in the town of Kolesniki, where my Grandfather Noah and Grandmother Esther Finkelstein maintained a fruit orchard that they had planted when they were young. A small stream bordered with trees and bushes flowed through the center of the orchard. Sweet cherries, yellow and red, hung from the tangled branches; miniature red radishes grew in the nearby garden. Hollyhocks covered the fertile ground of the large field like a carpet, and giant dahlias stuck out from among the hollyhocks. A small waterfall at the highest part of the garden was surrounded by colorful wildflowers. With its burst of color, the garden was beautiful to see, and on weekends and during summer vacations, all the family would gather there to enjoy it.

The town of Kolesniki was a well-known tourist attraction and drew sightseers from the entire area because of a unique mountain, which overlooked the edge of town. It was a tall mountain, made up of layer upon layer of wonderfully colored earth—yellow, orange, white, brown and red. The village girls would dig up the clay of the mountain and use it to create planters, pots and other objects filled with the colored sand. The Horyn River flowed near the town, and along both banks wheat fields sprawled, along with foliage, waterfalls and weeping willows. We children loved to walk along the banks of the stream and gather colorful pebbles. It was there, in that environment of breathtaking beauty, that I drank in my love of the earth and all growing things.

A dairy farmer lived near Grandfather's garden. He used to make cheese from the milk he got from his two cows. Every morning, Stefa, the farmer, would milk the cows. Grandfather wanted me to drink fresh milk, but I didn't like the foam and fat that rose to the top, so Grandfather would boil the milk and prepare hot cocoa for me. The milk was also used to make yogurt, sour cream and buttermilk, which were stored in the cellar in earthenware jugs.

The majority of household activities revolved around raising the children and preparing tasty dishes and food for the Sabbath and holidays. I remember the eve of the Passover seder at Grandfather Noah's house. Preparations began immediately after Purim. Plasterers would come to whitewash the house and paint the window sashes and doors. Aunt Sheindel Nissingoltz would arrive with her maid. The large kitchen would hum with activity as they scrubbed every corner of the house. They prepared wine in large casks that held up to five gallons each. They made the wine from raisins, and it fermented until a week before the holiday. We never had to buy horseradish; the stream that flowed through Grandfather's garden yielded enough to provide for the holiday.

Mother would also go to Grandfather's house to help with the Passover preparations. She would leave my two small brothers at home in Berezna, under the supervision of our good-hearted Domka. She would bring pots filled with goose fat, which she had prepared at the beginning of the winter. Matzoth smeared with *griven*, a mixture of goose fat and fried onions, was one of my favorite Passover foods.

We would beg Grandfather to open the big box of matzoth even before the holiday so he could spread them with goose fat for us. But Grandfather would say that it is forbidden to open the matzoth before the seder, and we had no choice but to wait impatiently for the holiday.

The maids would take down the special Passover cooking utensils from the attic, where Grandfather would store them during the year. These were ancient, passed down from generation to generation, decorated with beautiful pictures in bold shades of red and green and letters that combined to spell out the words "Happy Holiday," "Kosher for Passover," and "Elijah the Prophet." I remember Elijah's cup. It was silver, with intricate engravings and Hebrew letters, and I remember other pure silver bowls.

"Zeydele," I asked Grandfather, "Why do you hide these things?" And he answered, "I am hiding them from robbers. These utensils are very precious to me. They have been passed down in our family from generation to generation."

"What do you mean, Grandfather, 'from generation to generation'?"

"G-d willing, my little granddaughter Genya, when you grow up and get married, I will give you this silver bowl as a present. This is what 'from generation to generation' means. All of the granddaughters will receive something silver from me. I pray that I will be fortunate enough to live to see my granddaughters' weddings," he said with tears in his eyes.

"Grandfather," I asked him, "Why are you weeping?"

And he answered, "Because I get emotional when we speak of happy things." I promised Grandfather that I would grow up quickly and that he would be able to come to my wedding.

These utensils were the pride of our family tradition and were used on the holidays. We children loved to help wash them, but Father would become very angry any time we broke something. Nevertheless, we loved to touch those precious bowls, to wash them and to hold them in our hands. We felt we were touching our family history.

All the aunts and uncles and their children would come to Grandfather's house for the Passover holiday. In the morning of the holiday, Father would remove all the leaven and sell it to the Ukrainians. The parents would buy *pistachki* (peanuts) and many other kinds of nuts for the children to celebrate the holiday, and Grandfather Noah would buy all the grandchildren chocolate candies—kosher, of course, for Passover.

I was a very social and curious young girl and very friendly with the Polish and Ukrainian girls in the village. I loved to watch interesting things such as church weddings. But of course I never told Grandfather about that. I also used to go to watch the harvesting of the tall wheat stalks, along with my friend Tanya, who would invite me to visit her home in the village. Tanya's house was filled with holy Provoslavic icons, which were hung on the wall in a place of honor.

Tanya was a very bright girl. Once she asked me whether there was any truth to the rumor that we, the Jews, had murdered the Christian, Jesus. I didn't know who this

Jesus was, and she explained to me, "This is our holy man." She used to ask me about Jewish customs, and once she asked why my brother had been circumcised. I didn't know how to answer her questions, so I distracted her by suggesting that we go out to the fields. We walked there and gathered blue cornflowers, which grew in large quantities around the village, and we wove wreaths for our hair.

I loved eating at her home, but I was careful never to touch any pig's meat because Grandfather forbade it. Tanya tried again and again to understand the reason for this prohibition. But here also, I was not able to satisfy her curiosity. Years later, when she grew up and came to know her own mind, Tanya was swept up in the winds of hatred that engulfed the area, and she said that one day Hitler would come and kill all the Jews.

Grandfather Noah was in the wheat business along with Uncle Yankel, Father's brother. They also sold wheat to the owner of the mill, a Jew named Damon, a handsome and well-respected gentleman. Grandfather would send him sacks of wheat with the Ukrainian or Czech wagon drivers. Sometimes my brother Yossele and I would go with them to see how they ground the wheat and how the different kinds of flour, light and dark, were made. The mill was operated by water wheels powered by the river.

One day preparations began in honor of Uncle Itzik's upcoming marriage. I was then in the first grade. One cold winter day I returned home, my cheeks red from the cold, my hands in gloves, and I was startled at the sight of the wedding preparations. Everyone was there, hustling and bustling back and forth, moving from here to there.

Domka, Mother, Aunt Chayka and two more aunts, all of them busy baking cakes and preparing delicacies, fish, chickens and roasts.

"What is all this tumult? Why so much excitement?" I asked, and Mother answered that Uncle Itzik was getting married soon in the city of Kostopol, tens of miles from our village, and that we were all traveling to the wedding.

The wagon driver, Vermei, harnessed the horses to a big sled and loaded the food in large, empty wooden boxes that we used when we picked apples in our yard. They were bringing all these things to the bride's home. Is she really a *kallah*? I asked about the bride, for the word *kallah* in Hebrew can be interpreted as "bride" or as "lightweight." And, indeed, Uncle Itzik's bride was very heavy. She had a gigantic chest and swollen hands, and her face was so fat that I could barely see the slits of her eyes between the folds of skin. Uncle Itzik didn't want to marry her at all; he wanted to marry her younger sister. But the custom was that a younger sister could not marry before the older sister, so Uncle Itzik was forced to make do with the older—and heavier—of the two.

We traveled to the wedding in a sleigh hitched to horses. The bells on the horses' necks rang the entire way. The snow sparkled like crystal, and the sleigh left a black line in the road. Mother wrapped my brother Yossi and me in one of Grandfather's big fur coats so we would not freeze on the way. We all sat in a big basket called a *korzina*, with a down cover over us so we would be warm.

Mother wore a black fur coat with a silver-embroidered collar, which I loved to pat because it was so smooth and pleasant to touch. I wore a velvet dress, pleated at the hips, and a silk belt and new red shoes. From time to time, I would polish the shoes with my fingers so that they would shine.

After a long while we arrived at the place where the wedding would take place. There were lots of singers and entertainers there. The bride's parents were very wealthy, and the spread was enormous. The celebration lasted from the afternoon well into the night. My cousin, Shaya Rudiyak, the son of my mother's sister, Aunt Chayka, was already quite grown-up, but he enjoyed playing with us. He helped us build snow figures. We shaped a big groom, with black buttons from pieces of coal, and a bride with a sheet on her head, a shield on her face and paper flowers in her hands. The snow people were very successful, and because it was so cold they remained intact overnight. In the morning, Shaya built two new snow figures to complete the picture: a rabbi and a jester.

Father returned home the morning after the wedding, but we remained there several days longer with Mother.

Shortly afterwards I heard talk of a divorce. They were discussing Uncle Itzik and his bride, who refused to grant him a divorce. Itzik had fallen in love with a different young woman in Rovna, and the heavy bride's younger sister had already been married to someone else. "Only death will come between us," said Uncle Itzik's obstinate bride. And how right she proved to be.

three

Gloomy Skies

In September of 1939 the Poles left Berezna and were replaced by the Red Army. The Russians imposed a new order on our village. They disapproved of capitalist business owners and exiled many of them to Siberia. Siberia was considered a dreadful punishment, a curse in everyone's eyes. But much later it became clear that those who had been exiled to Siberia managed to survive the Nazis. The Russians were in control for a year and a half. In the middle of 1941, the Russian army left and the German army occupied our village. The retreating Red Army burned all its offices and documents when it left, leaving scorched earth behind them.

In the spring of 1938, a year before the arrival of the Russians, we were invited to the home of Aunt Sheindel and Uncle Levi Nissingoltz for the Passover seder. Their magnificent house, surrounded by an immaculate and meticulously maintained garden, was covered by climbing vines. Flowers sprouted from carefully cultivated earth. The trees blossomed, and the white blossoms of cherry, apple and pear trees blended wonderfully with the many colors of ornamental shrubs.

The seder took place in the elegant living room. Grandfather Noah Finkelstein and Father conducted it because Uncle Levi did not know much about religious matters. With the help of Domka and Aunt Sheindel's maid, Mother and Aunt Sheindel prepared wonderful delicacies that we all loved. The beautiful silverware was polished and shining, and everything sparkled and gleamed. The atmosphere was cozy and pleasant. Sheindel and Levi's children, who were grown-up and went to school in the city of Lvov, were there, and all the guests arrived with their arms full of gifts.

After the holiday Father returned to his business, and we remained there until the festival of Shavuot. It was a beautiful spring. The surrounding orchards were filled with fruit, and Father's business flourished. At the end of the summer, Father, Mother and Aunt Sheindel decided to travel together for a vacation in Kremnitz, a beautiful summer resort in a wonderful natural setting.

Aunt Gittel Finkelstein was not blessed with great wealth. She lived modestly with her husband, Shmilik Sodgalter, a carpenter, but their home was always clean and neat. When the Russians came in 1939, Shmilik was ecstatic. He was active in the Communist party and was well liked by the Russians. The arrival of the Red Army in Poland made the local Communists very happy. They greeted the Russians with bread, salt and floral wreaths, and spoke a strange, unintelligible language with them— Russian. But the Russians began making lists of "rich men" and "poor men," and the property owners, the "bourgeoisie," forfeited their property and were sent to Siberia.

We were also marked for deportation, as were my Aunt Chayka, her husband and her children.

As fate would have it, we were not sent to Siberia. Had we been, perhaps we all would have been spared. Mother and Aunt Chayka knew a Russian judge named Sharpilov, who was married to a Jewess. His wife, Mrs. Clara Sharpilov from Moscow, used to borrow evening gowns from Mother. She had no children but she was a warm-hearted woman and loved me and my little brothers. To the credit of Judge Sharpilov, we were somehow allowed to pay a fee instead of being sent to Siberia. Many other Jews were able to do the same.

As a young and very social girl, a loving child who had never known the meaning of the word "hatred" and who was friendly with Christian girls in the village, I suddenly began to experience the horror of anti-Semitism. Overnight, my Christian friends' attitude toward me changed. They and their brothers began to stone us with rocks, to hit us and shout, "Stinking Jews, go home!"

The fear and terror even penetrated Grandfather's peaceful home. It seemed as if the weeping willow trees wept for us and wailed about our bitter fate, and the beautiful waterfalls poured tears of sorrow and anguish upon us. From time to time children would go to pick sorrel to eat—wild sorrel grass, which grew abundantly on the banks of the small streams. Sometimes we searched for food because the supplies in Grandfather's house began to run out. And sometimes we tried to act as if life was as it used to be and nothing had changed. We continued picking wildflowers and weaving beautiful wreaths, especially from the blue cornflowers that bloomed among the wheat stalks. We wanted to forget about what was happening with the adults.

In 1941 when the Russians retreated, Uncle Shmilik Sodgalter picked up and left, going with them to Russia, abandoning Aunt Gittel and his daughters to the Nazis.

In June of 1941 the skies over our quiet home became overcast. On June 22 the Germans launched an aerial attack on the city of Kiev. At the same time the Germans invaded Poland and advanced as far as Volynhia. After several days rumors spread that they were burning villages and killing Jews. All at once fear and trembling replaced happiness and calm. The joy of childhood disappeared, and the burdens of adulthood suddenly settled upon us. Overnight I changed from a happy, smiling child to a mature young woman, experienced in suffering. At some point (I don't remember exactly when) Father met Russian partisans, and they suggested that he join them. Uncle Yankel also suggested escaping to Russia. However, Father refused to leave us behind. He hoped for the best. "We will yet be able to deal with these Germans," he said. And thus he sealed his own death sentence.

When the bombings began, we hid for a while in the cellar, where we had stored our food. We remained there for endless weeks with nothing to do, too fearful to go outside and worried about every stranger. The Germans formed Jewish labor crews and assigned them the task of cleaning up and repairing buildings that had been damaged or destroyed in the bombings. A decree was issued requiring all Jews over the age of ten to wear yellow patches on the chest and back, so that they could be easily identified as belonging to that despised group.

Many Jews fled from the main centers of Poland and arrived in our area. They came from Warsaw, from Lodz, from Tchenstochov and other places, and among them were some who stayed with us for different periods of time. Good-hearted Mother worked very hard, baking bread and preparing hot soup in large quantities for all these refugees, whom we called *Biazhinitza*. I remember the whispering between my parents and my uncle, Father's brother, about the terrible things the Germans were doing in occupied Poland. They spoke of escaping to Russia. Father and Mother were undecided but arrived at the conclusion that we were too young to be uprooted from place to place, and it was better that we remain at home. Obviously, they did not have the foresight to anticipate the magnitude of the approaching calamity.

We later learned that even in the first months after they conquered Volynhia, the Germans committed mass murder. In July and August of 1941, the Germans established fifteen ghettos in the area, and in 1942 they began to liquidate the Jews in the ghettos. They took them to the outskirts of the villages and towns and gunned them down into open pits. The living and the dead were buried together, and even those who managed an initial escape were caught and shot dead.

All stores and businesses belonging to Jews were marked clearly in front, an open invitation to vandals and Jew-haters to pour out their wrath when the opportune moment arrived. Jews were removed from all official positions in the government and local authorities, and many found themselves without any means of support.

I don't remember, and perhaps I do not want to remember, the terrible day when I realized that the blissful days of my childhood had vanished forever.

Life in the village grew more and more difficult. The Germans issued a string of decrees against the Jews. We were forbidden to leave our homes all night from 6:00 p.m. until 6:00 a.m. We became prisoners under house arrest in the cold and dark. Jews were also forbidden to travel from town to town. This decree effectively terminated all business ties the Jews had previously maintained. Among those affected, of course, was my father, whose fruit business had covered all the towns and villages of the region.

We decided to move to Grandfather Noah's home in the village of Kolesniki for a while until things calmed down. Uncle Yankel, his wife, Pessya, and their children, Manya and Dudie, also came to live with us in that village. The war had cut short Dudie's medical studies. We heard rumors that they were killing Jews in Ostra, especially the rich ones, after they robbed them of all their money and property. Rivkah was fearful for her natural father, who remained in Ostra, and for her young sister who lived with him, and she wanted to go to visit them. Mother sent me to accompany Rivkah so she would not have to travel alone. We both spoke Ukrainian and Polish fluently. Dressed as Ukrainian girls, we assumed that we would be able to go and return in peace, protected by these disguises. Grandfather's wagon driver took us to the train station, and we went from there by train to Ostra, a short distance away. At the station, Aunt Gittel was waiting for us with her two daughters. On the way to Rivkah's father's house, we saw many armed German soldiers and many Ukrainian militiamen. We were deathly afraid but continued walking, with frozen expressions on our faces.

We stayed in Rivkah's father's house and helped the family with the housework, the cleaning and the laundry. When several days had passed, Rivkah's fears were relieved, and we decided to return home. On the way back to Grandfather Noah's home in Kolesniki, we saw groups of Jews being detained by the Germans. The soldiers pulled the Jews' beards, and we tasted gall as we observed their shame. On the trip from Ostra to Kolesniki, armed soldiers suddenly stopped the train in order to check out the passengers. Militiamen boarded and went from car to car, searching for Jews. Rivkah was very frightened. She said that we should jump off the train. I had turned to stone from fear. "I can't," I told her. "My legs are truly paralyzed. Let's pretend to be Polish girls." But Rivkah said that her appearance would give her away. "They will see immediately that I am a Jew," she said fearfully, and she jumped from the train which was moving quite slowly.

I remained. My non-Jewish features, as well as the peasant dress I wore, apparently saved my life on that fateful trip. I traveled home from the train station by wagon. I held out my hand, and the good-hearted wagon drivers, whom I addressed in Ukraininan, took me as far as the village. Mother was waiting for us, dressed in an embroidered dress and looking like a local Christian woman. We took Grandfather's Ukrainian wagon driver and set off to look for Rivkah along the path the train had taken. We found her; her arms were broken, and her face and body were bruised. Mother said that I was a little hero, having withstood the test.

One day, Vladek the stutterer, Grandfather's neighbor from across the street, came over and warned us to run away quickly. "Ukrainians are searching for Jews and killing them without mercy," he told us excitedly. We didn't manage to escape. My brothers were small, and Mother was in shock. She held Leibele, my little brother, in her arms. Suddenly, in the middle of the day, Hungarian militiamen, together with Germans and Ukrainians with rifles and rubber clubs, burst into our home. They trampled the plants in the yard with their heavy boots. Several of them pounded on the door. They grabbed Father, Grandfather and my Uncle Yankel. They took them to the edge of the village and ordered them to dig pits for themselves. On the way they beat them brutally. We watched from the window and saw the three of them picking up cow and horse dung from the road with their hands and stuffing it into their yarmulkes. Afterwards, they cut off my Grandfather's beard and my Uncle Yankel's as well.

From the window we saw everything. They hit Father in his right eye. He never again saw through that eye. They also broke his nose and his teeth. My uncle was left in the field, unconscious and bleeding heavily. From then until the day of his death he remained lame and sickly. The entire time we remained locked in the room with Grandmother Esther, who lay as if paralyzed. Mother, my little brothers, my adopted sister, Rivkah, and I wept.

Toward morning the mayor of the village and his two

sons came and brought Grandfather, Father and Uncle home, barely alive. Grandfather and Grandmother embraced and wept. My heart was torn apart at the sight of their tears and of Grandfather's bruised face. We all decided that conditions had become too dangerous and that we had to hurry and run away from the village.

Father had buried the silverware and portable gold items in Grandfather's cherry orchard when the riots had begun, in anticipation of times of dire need—which had, in fact, arrived. One night I returned with Father to the cherry orchard. Father dug in the earth and removed the jewelry and money. Mother guarded the jewelry and money in a bag, which she had sewed from a linen towel and attached to the girdle she wore over her underwear. She always wore a wide skirt so that if she were to encounter robbers, "bandits," from among Stefan Bandera's thugs, they would not notice the bulging bag. At night Father would go out to find food. One night he returned home in total shock. He told us that the Ukrainians had slaughtered Grandfather Noah and Grandmother Esther with axes as they slept in their beds and buried them in the orchard among the cherry trees near the beds of radishes and carrots.

That night I saw, among the budding trees, a mound of earth resembling a large, round skullcap, covered by many hollyhock blossoms. But Grandfather was not there any longer. The cherry orchard had become a cemetery without a monument, with Grandfather and Grandmother buried in its earth. The sight of that flowering mound was forever imprinted upon my tender soul. There, under the cherry trees, a part of me was also buried.

I didn't believe that we could continue living this way,

in constant flight. I didn't believe we could continue to suffer like this. Was there no end in sight? My parents tried to raise my spirits. "There is no choice," Mother said to me. "Think of better times, which will surely come."

When we felt that the danger was also coming close to our home in the village, my parents decided that we had to run again, and whatever will be will be. We fled to Novostawsi, to friends of Grandfather near the forest of Novoselki, a distance of thirty to forty kilometers from the city of Rovna. We paid them a large sum of money, and they allowed us to stay in the storage shed in the yard.

Several days later rumors began to reach us from the surrounding villages that Jews were being imprisoned in ghettos. Posters in Ukrainian and German called for the Jews to return to their homes. "Nothing will happen," they were assured, and they were told they would be given jobs. This was a trick to round up the Jews in order to eliminate them. Many were deceived by the ruse and fell into the trap.

We saw danger all around us and realized that our situation had become very precarious. We decided to try to run away again. We could no longer escape to Russia. People trying to steal across that border were shot. Once again Labku, the mayor of Kolesniki, Grandfather Noah's friend, a noble-spirited gentile who had rescued many Jews, came to our aid. Labku, as his father before him, had served Tsar Nicholas as a wagon driver. He said that a wonderful family like the Finkelsteins must not be destroyed. Our family had lived in the village for generations. Even Grandfather Noah's grandfather had been born there. Labku came with his son, Padusio, a red-cheeked youth, and loaded us and our possessions onto his wagon. We traveled through the entire night. He said he had prepared a hiding place for us in straw-covered pits in the forest near the village.

We spent the first nights in a barn belonging to one of Labku's sons. Labku's wife shared with us the bread she had baked. One night she came running to the hut where we were hiding. We knew that a knock on the door in the middle of the night meant certain death. We were very frightened, but the mayor's wife calmed us. "I have only come to bring you hot soup," she said.

Conditions continued to worsen for the Jews remaining in the villages. Toward the end of the winter, all the trees had been cut down to heat the homes, and the supply of firewood had been used up. Because of the restrictions on traveling between villages, Jews could not gather wood from the forest, and their gentile neighbors were not eager to sell them firewood. It is very difficult to survive the brutally cold Ukrainian winters without heat. At times the temperatures reached thirty degrees below zero. Fences, storage sheds and barns were chopped up for firewood. Sometimes families would tear down their wooden homes to use the lumber for firewood, and they would go to live in the homes of friends or neighbors.

We had no hope at all of obtaining any heat. We lived in a yard, exposed to all the elements. Occasionally we came out of our hiding place to steal a bit of food that was left for the pigs and cows. Sometimes we managed to get bread and milk, which good-hearted gentiles gave us out of pity. The milk, of course, we gave to my little brothers. Leibele, my littlest brother, would scream from morning until night with hunger and cold, and we could not silence him. There were days when he burned with fever, and Mother stood by and wept, unable to help him. The problems continued to get worse. The hunger was like torture, and so was the fear that the Germans would discover our hiding place in the mayor's yard. We decided that we had to escape to the forest.

Once again we found ourselves living among the trees, changing our hiding place every day or two, hungry, filthy and suffering from the terrible cold. There in the forest we met Feigele, Father's cousin, the daughter of his aunt and of Srulik, Grandfather Noah Finkelstein's brother. Feigele, a young woman, had escaped from the Rovna ghetto with her husband, and the two had been living in the forest for quite some time. They had left their little daughter in the care of a Polish family in one of the small villages near the forest.

Feigele and her husband gave many valuable things to that Polish woman in exchange for keeping their little daughter. On one of the freezing winter days, Feigele, Rivkah and I went to visit Feigele's daughter. We took Mother's gold chain with us, the last piece of jewelry from all the jewels she had received from Father on their anniversaries. Mother had wanted to give this chain to Rivkahle on the day of her marriage. But in those dark days of cold, snow and hunger, she decided to try to exchange it for a bit of food from the Polish woman.

Rivkah and I stayed at the edge of the yard, and Feigele entered the house to meet with her little daughter. In a short time German soldiers, accompanied by

Ukrainians armed with rifles, surrounded the house. Rivkah and I managed to jump into a deep pit that held feed for the animals, sour beet greens, covered with straw. The Polish woman came running and heaped bundles of straw upon us to conceal us even more. We heard shots and screams. Feigele was killed as she held her small daughter in her arms, and their bodies were flung on the fence next to the pit where we were hiding.

Rivkah and I lay absolutely still in the pit, clutching one another under the rotting leaves and trembling from cold and fear. The slightest noise sounded to our ears like marching soldiers, coming to find us. We stayed this way until darkness fell, and at night we set out for the forest, to find Father and Mother. We walked all night, losing our way, and toward morning a snowstorm started, and we became totally disoriented. Suddenly, near the forest, we saw a solitary house, a miserable hut with smoke pouring from its chimney. Rivkah said that she remembered the cottage. "A good woman lives there, the one who once gave Mother bread and cheese without payment in return," she said to me.

It didn't seem to me that this was the home of that good woman, but I wasn't sure. We were frozen from the cold and very hungry. In the winter it is hard to find anything in the forest to relieve hunger, and we were forced to make a decision. Rivkah suggested that we go to the cottage. I was afraid to knock on the door, but Rivkah was a brave girl. She went in first, and I followed. It was immediately clear that we had made a mistake. There was a noisy group of drunken Poles in the house who rubbed their palms together gleefully when they caught sight of the fresh prey that had fallen into their hands. We tried to run away but they caught us, poured water over us (probably to clean away the beet silage) and, before we could understand what was happening, we were raped. I screamed, "I'm little, I'm little, leave me alone," but to no avail. They tore off our clothes and I felt that they were tearing me into little pieces. It was terrible. We were screaming and screaming. When it was over they urinated in our faces.

I did not exist. I thought that I would cease to be. I felt that I was dead. Then they left and we were left in the blood and urine and with the sense of this overwhelming filth, which did not leave me for many years. It was cold and we were wet. We found some torn sheets with which we covered ourselves and stumbled back to our parents' hiding place in the forest.

Mother saw us and immediately understood what had happened. She signaled us not to say a word since our father was broken and she did not want to add to his suffering. All that night the three of us sat huddled together, holding each other and weeping. That is what we did until morning.

Mourning and grief took over completely for all of us, especially Feigele's husband; his spirit had been broken. Father and Mother tried to comfort him, but he refused to be comforted about the loss of his wife and daughter. I remember that he used to repeat again and again that he had "lost his will to live." From time to time he would go out to search for food. He did not return from one of these expeditions; he simply vanished. Several days later Rivkah and I found his frozen corpse hanging from one of the trees in the forest. He left behind a brief letter addressed to my parents, but I never learned what it contained. For days afterwards I walked about as if I had been struck by lightning. I was haunted by the vision of the frozen corpse of that young man, who had been so devoted to his wife and daughter. I had loved him and had shared his pain. The memory of the sight of that frozen corpse hanging on the tree will be with me all the days of my life.

four

—

Blood and Death

It became more and more difficult to obtain food and clothing. One morning I awoke in the pit, my teeth chattering, almost frozen from the cold. Mother was at a loss about what to do. All of us were about to freeze to death. With the anguish of a young girl, I observed that the red sweater I loved so much, a present that my cousin Manya from Warsaw had given me for my birthday, was becoming old and worn. Mother cut the sweater in half and wrapped it around my frozen legs. Above the shreds of the sweater she tied on a pair of galoshes, which were already ripped and worn. The snow drenched my legs and made them freeze. My sister, Rivkah, "inherited" some meager articles of clothing from Feigele when she died, and my little brother received the clothing of her poor, murdered daughter—adorable girl's clothing knitted from high-quality angora wool, bought in the days when the sun still shone in our lives. Father wore the few items of clothing left behind by Feigele's husband, but Father was a tall man, and the clothes were too short for him. They hung on him as on a scarecrow because he had lost so much weight and his body had become so terribly thin.

With the coming of spring 1942, nature began to revive. Mother went with Rivkah to search for food, and when she returned I saw joy in her face. Her face shone, a sight I had not beheld for so long. The light of hope was reflected there. She told Father that as she had wandered about with Rivkah they had come upon a "colony" of Czechs in Novostawsi, about ten kilometers from Kolesniki. The good-hearted band had given Mother plenty of prepared food, milk and cheese. And they had also showered her with words of encouragement. "Soon the Russians will win, and the Germans will leave," they told her. "You are Jews; continue holding on to your hope. You will overcome this. You are only one unfortunate family among many. May you merit salvation and deliverance." This is what Mother told Father. Rivkah and I were ecstatic. We began to be swept away on the wings of our fantasies. In our minds' eye we saw the wonderful day when our parents would go to buy us new clothing and shoes, and we would also have as much chocolate as we could eat, and we would return to school. Father said that we would go to Palestine, "a land filled with sunshine and oranges."

Approximately two weeks later I went with Mother to find food. Each time we would sneak into a different area. Rivkah remained in our bunker to care for my little brothers and Father. We reached a village occupied by people who were well known for their extreme anti-Semitism. Mother lost her way, and we didn't know how to return to our bunker. This time we met with little success in finding food. Doors that had previously been open to us were slammed shut in our faces. "Get out of here, you accursed, stinking Jews!" they yelled at us. "What a pity they didn't kill all of you." We met with this reception in village after village. In one small Ukrainian town we were given bread and cheese, potatoes and hot soup. "Hurry, so the neighbors should not see you," the kind-hearted farmer woman said to us. "Be very careful. Bandera's Ukrainian youth brigades are in the area. May the good God bless you so that you don't run into them. They are real murderers. I bless you and wish you Godspeed. May our lord Jesus protect your souls."

We had just set out when a group of gentiles attacked us. They beat us and stole the food we had gotten. "You Jews are only waiting for the Russians to come so you can slander the Poles and Ukrainians who cooperated with the Nazis!" They ignored Mother's pleas and her words. "We are only seeking a bit of food for our small children in the forest," she said. We returned to the bunker empty-handed. Father had been very worried about us and knew in his heart that some misfortune had come upon us. Today I believe that it was that group of youths who betrayed us later and told the Ukrainians that we were hiding in the forests of Novoselki.

It was difficult to start a fire in our forest hiding place because in the spring the snows melted and soaked the branches and twigs. When we managed to light some coals, we roasted potatoes or beets. From time to time we prepared *makucha,* a hard lump made from seed husks used for cow's feed, a nourishing enough food, but difficult to obtain.

Our last spring was filled with hope. Many flowers

bloomed and covered the forest's bald patches with a thick white carpet. The fields surrounding us were plowed; I reminisced upon the blissful years of my childhood, and I thought that soon everything would return to how it used to be, and these dreadful days would be erased from our memory forever.

There were nights when we hid in a straw-covered pit that had been prepared for us in advance. Between the periods of hiding there were periods of calm, during which we returned to live in Grandfather Noah's brick house beside his cherry orchard.

Father was a religious man but not a fanatic. He did not have a beard, but every morning he would pray and put on tefillin, even in the forest. Even in the difficult times we endured he did not forget the Jewish holidays and festivals. One time when we were hiding in the forest in a cellar filled with mice and rats, he somehow managed to find oil and potatoes. He carved out holes in the potatoes and tore up some of his clothing so he could pull out cotton threads. "Why are you ripping that, Father?" I asked. And he replied, "It is faded and torn anyway, and today is Chanukah. We must light candles." Among the mice and rats, one of which bit my little brother on the nose, Father lit those candles made of potatoes and cotton wicks. He made the blessing and wept. This was the last holiday that we celebrated together.

Mother, who was fair-haired like a gentile, used to leave our hiding place in the forest to bring us food. Sometimes she would sell something from the house and receive a paltry sum of money that was enough to provide us with food for a few days. Father lay feebly, without the strength to move. The entire burden of maintaining our existence rested on Mother's shoulders. On one of our expeditions into the forest we met several Jewish families who had fled their homes in the area, among them, Yankel, Father's brother, his wife, Pessya, and their children, Manya and Dudie. After several weeks they left us, going off in another direction on their way to the home of a certain farmer, a friend who promised to hide them. On the way there they were caught by the Ukrainians, who cruelly attacked them with axes. All of them were slaughtered except for my cousin Dudie, who managed to escape. Once more we were struck by bitter news, and Father had great difficulty absorbing the magnitude of the tragedy. Our terror intensified. Death drew nearer and nearer. We feared that any moment they would find us.

And indeed the day came when we, too, were caught. The Ukrainians searched tirelessly for Jews. No doubt, if not for the overwhelming hatred the Ukrainians had for the Jews, the Germans would never have achieved such success in eliminating the Jews of Poland. Day after day the Ukrainians would go with their dogs from house to house, from barn to barn, from shed to shed, until in the end they found us, too. When they discovered us, they loaded us on a wagon with other Jews gathered from the nearby yards, and we were moved to the ghetto in our village of Berezna. I remember the ghetto as being extremely crowded, a place of terrible filth, lice, disease and especially, the most awful fear.

The *aktions* (round-ups of Jews) and the liquidations

began. In one of the *aktions* we were smuggled out of the ghetto by a friend, a farmer woman. Most likely she was paid handsomely from whatever assets we had left. She hid us in a wagon full of hay and took us to the forest. We found ourselves once again in a cold and damp pit, filthy, hungry and afraid, but we had escaped by the skin of our teeth. For indeed, one day at 4:00 a.m. the Germans assembled the majority of the Jews of the ghetto in Berezna's village square. They took them to the outskirts of the village, shot them and threw them into three gigantic pits near the Polish school on the road to Malynsk.

Once more the winter returned, and with it the frost. Our clothing was not enough to protect us from the cold. Mother wrapped our legs in rags and tied them with ropes because our shoes had fallen apart. She had managed to get a pair of galoshes for herself, a real find in those days, and someone had given her woolen socks. Every morning she would risk her life and go from door to door, begging for a bit of food for us.

One day she did not return until very late. When she arrived, she could not stop crying for hours. She sighed and moaned the entire night; her clothing was stained with blood. Later I learned that she had been raped by a band of Ukrainians, and after they had abused her, they set their dogs upon her, the dogs they used to search for Jews.

After that Mother lay in the pit for many days without venturing outside. There was no one to get food for us. We were literally on the threshold of death from starvation. Even the *makucha*, the cow feed made of seed husks that we used to dip into water and eat, was used up.

Father no longer had any choice. Weak and sick, he would sneak into the farmers' yards at night and steal rotten potatoes which had been set aside to feed the pigs.

One night he returned badly bruised. A horse had broken out of one of the stalls and kicked him in the back. Then he had lost his way in a snowstorm and only returned to us with the greatest difficulty, crawling back to the pit. His injured eye pained him greatly. My little brothers suffered from bleeding hemorrhoids. All winter my parents struggled to gather branches and boards that they found nearby to protect us from the cold and the snow. We could not light a fire for cooking or for warmth or even prepare tea from the herbs we found in the forest, because the smoke would give us away. Thus life went on, amidst suffering and sickness, until the spring.

In the spring many nettles began to bloom. We ate nettles and the potatoes that we stole. Sometimes Mother would disguise herself as a gentile woman and go around to the nearby homes, begging for milk for my little brothers. To prevent our being discovered again, we decided to change our hiding place in the forest frequently. For days on end we marched along narrow paths, stooped over in single file, the thick underbrush hiding us from view. Father always went first, and we followed. We lost all sense of time. All our attention was focused upon the children, to feed them and keep them as healthy as possible. In a moment of despair, Mother decided to leave my little brother Leibele, who was sick and constantly crying, to the kindness of a local farm wife, a good-hearted gentile who took pity on the sickly baby and agreed to care for him. We left him crying and went on our way. We continued walking and had covered quite a distance, but I couldn't bear the thought that we were abandoning my brother. My heart broke inside, and I began to cry.

"I will take care of him," I promised my mother. We returned to the place where we had left him. He was sleeping peacefully, his thumb in his mouth. From a distance it appeared as if he were no longer breathing. Perhaps he had begun to freeze. Mother hurried to feed him a grayish white liquid, perhaps water mixed with milk, and he began to make some sounds and to mumble. I gathered him to me with great emotion, and I cried. Then I took him and carried him on my back. On that sad day I swore we would never again be parted, that only death would come between us.

For a while Gittel and her daughters hid with us in the forest after her husband, Shmilik, the carpenter, had abandoned them and fled by himself to Russia. In those days we would hide in the distant forest, about thirty kilometers from Ostra. The Germans had posted notices all over Ostra declaring that anyone willing to leave the ghetto to work would receive food. Many people were persuaded to do this; they left the ghettos and were killed immediately by the Germans. For some reason Gittel decided to return with her daughters to the Ostra ghetto. During one of the *aktions*, her three daughters were killed, along with hundreds of other young girls. Aunt Gittel herself died sometime later in the ghetto. "Who knows," I have thought time and again since then, "maybe if they had remained in the forest with us, they would be alive today."

We continued living in the forest, wandering from place to place because the area was being combed frequently and thoroughly for Jews. One day my parents raised the idea of going to the priest, Ilchuk. Ilchuk was a Baptist, a dear man, well known for his love for his fellow human beings. He did not differentiate between Jews and Christians. He simply loved all people. He hoped that he would be blessed for helping Jewish families by finally realizing his dream of going to the Holy Land, Palestine, sacred to Christians as well as Jews.

So one rainy Friday evening, soaked to the marrow of our bones, my two little brothers burning with high fevers and shivering with cold, my parents decided to approach Kolesniki, where the priest lived. "Maybe we can hide there in the granary, among the hay stored for the animals," they said. We continued walking. As usual, we followed a path hidden by the thick forest overhang, which by now we knew well. Suddenly a great and sudden fear seized us. On the slope parallel to us we saw a figure with a rifle on its shoulder. Several times we stopped. The figure halted as well. In my imagination I saw the German soldiers swarming all over us, grabbing my little brother, who was asleep in my arms with his head resting on my shoulder. I was paralyzed by fear and I couldn't move. "Come, let's run away," I mumbled, but Mother answered coolly, *"Drei nisht mein kop, gay veiter"* (Don't drive me crazy, keep going!). Soon we were swallowed up by the green foliage and were hidden from view.

After a steady and exhausting march, we reached Ilchuk's house. We knocked on the door, fearing the reception. His wife opened the door. We stood there silently, dressed in tatters, trembling with cold and fear. With great compassion, the woman welcomed us into the house, offering us fresh bread and warm milk.

I devoured the food, the likes of which I had not seen for so long. I ate and ate and could not be satisfied until finally my stomach was full. The priest arrived after we had filled ourselves and seemed not at all surprised by our sudden appearance at his home. He was quiet as usual, his prayerbook in hand. He told us that the war would end soon and that all of us, including his extensive family, would travel to Palestine. He knew, he said, that he would be treated royally by the Jews in return for his efforts in saving so many lives. He spoke for a long time about his longing for Jerusalem, the holy city. Afterwards he invited us to wash up in his home. The Ilchuk couple heated water for us, and we washed in the wooden washtub. It had been many weeks since we had changed our clothes, so this was a very emotional and totally wonderful experience for us. We scrubbed the children, one after another, and washed their heads with kerosene because of the lice that infested their hair. Afterwards we sat in the warm guest room, and the priest, Ilchuk, read to us about "The New Covenant." Father clutched his talit and siddur in his hand. Mother's face expressed hope, and she said that soon the war would be over, and the Russians would come, and we would all go to Palestine.

Several hours later they took us to the shed in the yard, where we were to sleep. Our rest was sweet and pleasant that night. It had been so long since we had gone to sleep with full stomachs, scrubbed and clean. It was as if we had been prepared to meet our deaths. Or maybe it was just fate mocking us one final time.

I fell asleep at once, covered with an old blanket, which to my eyes appeared to be a magnificent quilt. In my dream I saw a horse trampling on Grandfather and Grandmother's graves, with the horse's hooves on the mound of dust in the yard of their house, in the cherry orchard that I had loved so much. I tried to save them but couldn't. I wanted to call to Mother for help but couldn't manage to make a sound. I wanted to extend a hand to Grandfather Noah, but I couldn't. Even that day I realized that the dream about Grandfather Noah was what saved my life. I, who in my dream wanted so much to rescue Grandfather Noah from the horse's hooves, was saved in his place. That dream comes back to me frequently, even today, at the moment of reciting *Yizkor*, the memorial prayer for the dead, as well as during difficult times and sleepless nights, and in my nightmares.

I woke up terrorized from that frightful dream to hear dogs barking as they approached the shed, and immediately I heard shouts in German and Ukrainian. At first I didn't know if I was dreaming or if it was really happening. Shots were being fired on all sides. I heard Mother shouting and pleading in Ukrainian, "Take pity on the little ones," she cried. "They are innocent!" Her voice shook. I heard my little brothers crying. I could barely see in the darkness except for flashes of light from flashlights. Some force that I will never be able to understand caused me to vault over the wooden fence that separated the shed and the nearby pigsty. I jumped into the trough, amid the mud and the mire, and then I heard shots. Afterwards all was still.

Filthy with the mud and the dirt, I arose and ran, realizing that I was still alive, to the nearest house, the home of Ilchuk's son. I knocked hard on the door and it opened. I begged the priest's son to let me in, that they were killing us! He pushed me out and said, "We have enough trouble because of you Jews. Get out of here! And anyway, my wife is in labor." The door slammed shut on my hand. I began to run, but I didn't know where. I ran, and I heard shots behind me. I was struck in the right hip. I fell and lay there without moving, from pain and fear.

The murderers reached me. I lay silent, biting my lips in pain and restraining myself from making a sound. They kicked my back and my head and shook me. One Ukraininan said that I was dead. Afterwards there was silence. Apparently I had fainted. I don't know how long I lay that way. Time passed. Afterwards I pulled together the strength to get up and begin walking. I didn't know where I was going. I only knew that I wanted to run far away from there. I walked without looking back, my main objective to get away, to run far, far away from there. I was gripped with fear. From time to time I fell, and apparently I slept or lost consciousness again.

When I awoke I found myself covered with dirt and drenched with blood. I stank of blood mixed with sweat and was so thirsty I thought I would die. Every so often a wave of nausea overcame me, and my head would swim. I decided that I was going back, no matter what, to the priest Ilchuk's house, to Father. "It is not possible that Father is dead," I told myself again and again. "No one can overcome him. Not my father. He is probably alive and waiting for me to return." My thoughts became confused as I tried to remember exactly what had happened. I tried to remember the events of the past two days and couldn't. It required tremendous spiritual reserves and a heart of steel to survive and remember my dear mother's last words, as she pleaded with the murderers to take pity on her little children.

I struggled to reach the priest's home, alternately walking and crawling, and before evening I arrived there once again. His wife was shocked to see me. I seemed like a ghost to her. The children ran away and hid, my appearance was so frightful. She gave me a piece of bread and some milk. I tried to eat but could not. I vomited everything I put in my mouth. I trembled with fear and hunger.

I asked to see my parents. The priest's wife seemed at a loss. "Poor girl. Don't you know they killed them all there?" she said, gesturing with her hand. "Their corpses were right there before we buried them in one grave." I burst out in tears. "Maybe they killed the children," I said over and over, "but they could not have killed my father. My father is big and strong. They could not kill him."

But the priest's wife showed me Father's talit, which was stained with blood, and told me that they themselves had buried my parents and my three brothers and my adopted sister, Rivkah, in the forest, in the clothing and blankets that had covered them when they died. She herself had almost collapsed at the fearful sight, and her husband the priest had told her to remain in the house until he burned all the blood-covered straw in the shed. The Ukrainian militiamen commanded the priest and his wife to clean everything up so there should be no sign of what had happened there. Then the Ukrainians returned and carried out another search. They said that according to the information they had received, one girl was missing. It appeared they had received information from the Ukrainian neighbors. They warned the Ilchuk family that they would burn their home if I returned and they helped me. The priest's wife urged me to hurry and wash up; she bandaged my wound, supplied me with bread and fat and begged me to leave quickly because they were liable to return at any moment. I tied a kerchief on my head, and in the white cotton dress she gave me I looked like a Ukrainian girl. She blessed me, warned me not to talk to anyone and not to tell what had happened to me. She made me swear that I would try to smile and not to cry. "God will be with you," she said and sent me on my way.

I walked the entire night. When I turned toward the area of Novostawsi, I passed near a farm settlement of wealthy Czech farmers. On the way I remembered that the owner of one of the farms was Mrs. Gayevska, a veterinarian, and that she had been a friend of Grandfather Noah Finkelstein, and her husband had done business with Grandfather and Father. I remembered that she was a good woman who always helped people in need. Without hesitating I knocked on the door. In a few moments it opened a crack, and Mrs. Gayevska peered through. When she recognized me she appeared frightened and drew me inside quickly. I told her briefly what had happened. I could not supply her with details. Silently she motioned for me to follow her, and she took me to a cold and dark cellar where she stored potatoes and carrots.

I saw two cats there whose job, apparently, was to protect the food from mice. The mice, however, seemed to roam there without fear. A sliver of pale daylight came through a small window on the upper portion of the wall, which allowed for some ventilation. The mistress of the house begged me not to go up into the house because her two grandsons were liable to arrive suddenly, and she knew, from their own account, that they had participated in the murder of my family. Former students at the Polish gymnasium in Rovna, they had hated Jews since their earliest childhood. This had been a golden opportunity for them to exterminate the surviving members of the last Jewish family in the area. They had told her gleefully how they had cruelly murdered my little brothers, and she, their grandmother, had not been able to influence them to change their ways. They continued to search for Jews in the surrounding area. In an unguarded moment, Mrs. Gayevska also told me that this same gang had murdered Bayla, Father's sister, and her daughters.

Mrs. Gayevska told me that the villagers had gathered at the church and declared the area to be "Jew free." She strongly denounced the crowd and expressed her sorrow that these kinds of Ukrainians had succeeded. "I couldn't help the dead," she said, "but my heart weeps when I am reminded of your parents. I remember I was a guest at their wedding. Your mother looked like an angel, with her green eyes and bright hair. She looked just like a Christian! Now you are all alone. Come, I will tend your wound or you will die of infection." She spread an ointment on my wound, and at night I was allowed to go into the house to wash up. When she saw that I had lice, she washed my hair with kerosene.

I stayed in Mrs. Gayevska's cellar five days and five nights. Thoughts about my dead family tormented me constantly. Before the weekend she asked that I leave at once because one of the neighbors had seen me through the window when I came into the house, and she feared that he would tell the Ukrainian militia that I was there. She said there was also a chance that her grandsons would go down to the cellar when they came to visit on Sunday, and they would surely kill me.

When I finished packing my few belongings, she gave me some clothing, wrapped up some bread and cheese for the trip and directed me to walk toward the village of Babin. She suggested that I try to approach her son-in-law, Omelko, principal of the local school, who had also been a friend of our family. She told me that he had many Jewish friends, and she remembered that he used to love the food Mother would prepare for the Sabbath. She told me that Omelko had told her often about the wonderful gefilte fish and delicious strudel my mother had served him.

five

Hard Times

I went on my way. Once again I trudged down the roads, heading nowhere in particular. I stopped at the home of a gentile woman named Farasca, who was the owner of a large orchard. I remembered that Father and Grandfather used to buy fruit from her wholesale. In the days of the Polish regime, before the arrival of the Russians, she would visit our home to conduct her business. She was quite a wealthy woman. When they began herding the Jews into the ghetto, we had succeeded in smuggling out many valuable items to her home: expensive furs, silverware, Mother's jewelry and even velvet coverlets. She had promised that she would care for everything until the turmoil was over.

She greeted me warmly. It seemed she already knew that my entire family had been murdered. Without my asking, she promised that I could stay in her home for a while. "I remember Grandfather Noah's kindness in days gone by," she said. "And you are good Jews and not swindlers like the other Jews in the village who were dishonest with weighing the wheat and fruit." In a whisper she told me that a short time before, my cousin Dudie had stayed overnight in her home, that he had also escaped and was in hiding. I didn't have the strength even to thank her. I fell fast asleep in the small kitchenette where feed for the pigs was prepared.

I woke up to the sound of dogs barking and someone knocking at the door. I was gripped by fear. "Now," I said to myself, "they are coming to kill me. This time my end has surely come. There is nowhere to run." I trembled with fright. As if carved in stone, I remained seated in my place. A few moments later, Farasca entered, followed by my cousin Dudie. We fell into each other's arms, crying and overcome by a torrent of emotion. We could not speak. Dudie remained with me the entire night. We sat in the small, dark kitchenette, and I told him with great anguish about all the horrors I had endured. He told me that his parents and his sister, Manya, had also been killed in the same area.

A few hours later, at dawn, Farasca requested that Dudie leave her home. "Soon they will come here to look for Jews," she said. They will strip you of your pants and see that you are a Jew. You'd best leave before daylight." Before we parted, Dudie convinced me not to remain there in hiding but to continue on my way. He advised me to go to the village of Babin and to say there that I was one of the orphans from the orphanage in Kiev. He told me to say that I did not remember my parents and that I had no idea where they were, but that I knew for sure that they were pure Ukrainians. "It is worthwhile," he told me, "to make it a habit of genuflecting every morning," and he taught me a prayer in Ukrainian. "I warn you once again," he said.

"Don't say a word about your family and your experiences. When you grow up, and these horrors pass, you will be able to find a city with Jews to tell about our murdered family and to avenge their blood. Genyaleh," he said again. "You must prevail. Search for work as a field hand or a nanny." He knew that he himself had no hope. His fate was sealed. And indeed, a short while later he was captured by the men of the Ukrainian and German militia and hung. I learned this after the war, in 1945, from Farasca herself.

Meanwhile I stayed with Farasca. One day I became feverish with a high temperature. I was overcome with severe coughing fits and chills. Farasca had no choice but to call Marinka, the doctor, and apparently her friend, to attend me. "This is from the wound on your hip," Marinka said. The wound looked awful; it was oozing a great deal of pus and giving off a putrid odor. Marinka was a shaman healer, and the countrywomen in the area believed with all their hearts in her powers. She tended me with devotion and rubbed ointments, which she herself concocted, on my wound. I continued to burn with fever for several days. I could eat nothing and drank only herbal teas. Finally I recovered. But in the meantime Marinka had told her daughter that a young Jewess was being hidden by Farasca, and Ukrainians on horseback arrived at the house to capture me and hand me over to the Germans. Luckily Farasca learned of this in time. She helped me escape to the forest in a wagon filled with hay. In the forest she had me get out of the wagon and said angrily, "Go and don't come back any more, or they will kill me, too. I've had enough of you Jews. It's not worth my dying over a *Zhidovka perchata* (a

Jewess with ringworm)." Once again I was seized with deadly fear. I was terrified of the beasts in the forest and of the human beasts who were stalking me.

I fell asleep and woke up toward morning. A huge fox stood near me. I didn't move. He sniffed me, apparently attracted by the stench of the wound and the smell of the cheese I held. He began to draw closer to me. I jumped away and quickly climbed one of the trees. I sat on a branch and waited a long time. Finally I threw the cheese at him, and he took it and left. From a distance I spotted a convoy of uniformed Ukrainians and Germans, making their way down the dusty roads. I heard them singing in Ukrainian. I knew that the hour of my death was near. And I didn't even care. Quite the contrary, death suddenly seemed a simple way out of all my troubles, a solution to the problem of my miserable existence and my constant fear.

"I don't want to continue living like this," I said to myself. "I have no strength. Maybe I'll run toward them," the thought occurred to me. "I'll tell them that I am a Jewess and bring an end to all my woes." I began walking toward them in my white, embroidered dress. When I drew near, they spoke to me in Ukrainian, asking who I was. Suddenly I did not want to die. I wanted to live very much. "They call me Jenia," I answered in my excellent Ukrainian. "I come from Kiev." "Where do you live?" they asked me. "I have no home," I responded. "I come from an orphanage. A man brought me here and told me they are looking for girls to work in the field or to care for young children." They whispered among themselves and let me continue on my way.

I felt as if a great weight had been lifted. Suddenly I rejoiced that I was alive, that they had not killed me after all. I sat by a brook at the side of the road. I ate some of the bread and drank some water from the brook. I dipped my aching feet in the water. I noticed deep cracks had been carved into the soles of my feet. Afterwards I continued walking until evening fell. When it grew dark I met a farmer, and I asked him the way to Babin. "Why do you want to go to Babin?" he asked. "I have heard there is a sugar factory there and that they are looking for girls to work," I responded. We began to talk. Once again I told my fictional story, and when I said that I was an orphan tears welled up in my eyes. The farmer was touched by my words, and he invited me, the Ukrainian orphan girl, to spend the night in his home.

It was a cozy and pleasant home. Many children sat around the large wooden country table. I envied them their light hair and blue eyes. I so wanted to resemble them, to be a gentile, to look like them, to *be* one of them.

The table was full to overflowing. I sat, confused and filled with jealousy at being with this warm and amiable family. I tried to mask my hunger and to eat little and politely. Before going to bed I was given a glass of delicious warm milk, and I was sent to sleep in a small room with the farmer's daughters. I woke at daylight. After eating breakfast, I genuflected and pronounced a blessing. It was apparent that the farmer was impressed by this. He gave me some bread, meat and fruit and showed me the road leading to Babin.

Once again I was on the move. I walked and walked.

I had no idea how long I walked and how much distance I covered. When I became very tired, I sat down to rest in a wheat field. Sheaves of grain stood in the field, but I managed to find a quiet corner where I could sit and eat. I could not continue walking. I fell asleep and slept until the next morning. I woke up to the sound of farmers talking as they harvested the wheat. They approached me and asked what I was doing. With half-closed eyes, I repeated my story. One of them was suspicious. He commanded me to rise and open my eyes. He looked straight into them and asked, *"Ty Zhidovka?"* (Are you a Jewess?). Immediately I crossed myself and said, "How absurd! I am Ukrainian. My name is Jenia Stepaniyuk, daughter of Katya Stepaniyuk." He stared into my eyes again and said, "You have the eyes of a Jew." I remembered what my cousin had taught me. I pulled together my courage, looked directly at him and said that my father might have come from Uzbekistan. I did not remember him. But my mother was a Ukrainian from the city of Kiev. After a few moments they left me and returned to their work.

It was summer. The forest was full of fruit: blackberries, raspberries and strawberries. I ate the bread I had and picked fruit, and I continued searching for the main road leading to Babin. Far away I saw people and vehicles moving. I walked in that direction and reached the main road. Convoys of vehicles, many German ones among them, moved along the highway. I noticed some wagons carrying Ukrainian girls who had been drafted to help out the Germans in a variety of jobs. I feared that I would be taken into one of those wagons and that in the end my origins would be revealed. I didn't know how long I could continue to hide my identity.

The sky grew dark, and it began to rain. I had walked a long time and was tired. I turned to look for a house or shed to hide in. I was drenched to the bone, and the wound on my hip was very painful. I saw a house not too far away. It was the village of Taikuri. A large, vicious dog was chained in the yard, and he was pacing back and forth in front of the house. I was afraid to approach. With my last strength, I called out to the owners of the house to let me come in. A blue-eyed farmer with a threatening face came out of the house and asked what I wanted. I said that I was a refugee from Kiev, an orphan, that my mother had been killed in the bombing raids, and that I was on my way to Babin, to the sugar factory there, to look for work. He believed my story and even invited me to stay and have dinner with his family. Once again I was lucky to find a warm home and a hot meal. At the table I heard some friends of the family, among them the priests of the Ukrainian village church, say that a Jewish family in hiding had been discovered in the attic of an abandoned house. "It's good that they caught and killed them all," they all said. "Now we can sleep in peace. we are rid of those Jewish parasites."

It's possible that I turned pale, because suddenly all eyes became riveted on me, and the whispering began. I saw them inspecting my face. The head of the household asked me once again if I were truly Ukrainian, and how did I remember who and what I was. I was reminded suddenly of a poem by the Ukrainian poet Taras Shevchenko, which I had memorized in third grade. I recited the poem from memory with no trace of a foreign accent. At the conclusion of the meal I genuflected and thanked them.

That night I could not fall asleep. I feared that at any moment one of them might betray me to the Germans. At dawn I arose, got dressed and prayed. I thanked them and made my departure, continuing my trip. Every so often I stopped and looked back, fearing someone was chasing me.

I reached Babin after walking a full day. From a distance I saw a window of the sugar factory. Joy and hope came back to me and gave me strength. "Maybe now I will be rescued from my wanderings and afflictions," I said to myself. My purpose now was to find Mr. Omelko, the principal of the school, who had been a friend of my family. Some years ago we had visited the Omelko family's gracious home. The house was surrounded by a flower garden with a waterfall and big trees. I hoped he would let me be a maid in his home.

It began to grow dark, and I lost my way. I turned toward the main road and decided to ask for directions at one of the homes. I knocked on the door of one of the houses that had a sign, "Kill all the Jews! Clean up Ukraine!" An attractive woman stood at the door. When I asked if I could spend the night, she agreed and offered me food and drink. In the morning she surprised me with a dress, and I started walking in the direction she showed me. In the distance I saw the school and the principal's home next door.

I knocked on the door. Mrs. Omelko, elegantly dressed, opened the door and asked what I wanted. I answered with confidence, "I have heard that the school principal is seeking a young girl to help out in the house." She inspected me carefully and called her husband, who was relaxing in the dining room, enjoying a festive Sunday dinner with guests. When he saw me, he appeared dumbfounded. At first he was silent. Then he told me to come into a side room. I was confused. After several moments, which felt like an eternity to me, he entered and said, "My poor girl. I know everything about the murder of your family. You must not tell my wife that I was a frequent guest at your home. She will betray you to the Germans without hesitation. She hates Jews and has become friendly with the Germans." According to him, the sons of his wife's sister had taken part in the murder of my family. It became clear to me that Principal Omelko's wife was Mrs. Gayevska's daughter and the aunt of the murderers. "They visited here not long ago and spoke with pride about how they threw the corpses on the fence," he told me. Afterwards he said that we should maintain a lot of formality in our relationship, and he instructed me to address him as "Master Principal" and his wife as "Mistress Principal."

"You will be able to work for us and remain here a while," he added. "But my wife's family visits us every few weeks on Sundays, and therefore you must take care to disappear from the house on those days. They are looking for Jews who are still alive, and they murder them without mercy. On Sunday mornings, go to church to pray," he said. "After services, go to the Czech neighbors. There is a young girl there named Stefa. Become friendly with her and stay with her until late in the evening. When the guests leave I will call you to return home."

Mrs. Omelko treated me with utter disdain. She told me that she hated strangers and fed me leftovers that were to be used for feeding the pigs. When she was out of the house the principal would sit me down at the kitchen table, which she forbade me to approach, and he would feed me on household delicacies.

Several weeks passed. One morning when I was in the field not far from the house, busy picking strawberries, Mr. Omelko called me and told me that I must go to a family near the sugar factory, tell them that he sent me to them and stay with them for a while. When he saw that I didn't understand, he explained in a whisper, "Guests are expected to arrive here, among them the mayor of the village and important Germans from the local headquarters, as well as my wife's two nephews, who are known to be ruthless Jew-killers. They are liable to recognize you." He added that he would tell his wife that he had sent me away because he wanted an older girl.

I had no choice. I took my belongings in silence and, following Mr. Omelko's instructions, walked over to Maria and Petro's house, which was nearby. They were a young couple who owned a beautiful farm that they had inherited from Maria's parents. Maria's father was killed by the Russians in 1939 because he opposed the Communist regime. Her mother passed away a short time after. Maria was a pampered, only child, a graduate of the Polish gymnasium in Rovna, and she behaved like a royal princess. Her husband, Petro, was a good-hearted man but a Jew-hater since the days when he had worked as chief butcher in a restaurant owned by a Jewish family in the city of Lvov. The family was killed immediately after the Germans arrived. Petro belonged to a group of Ukrainians who were fighting for Ukrainian independence.

When I arrived at the house, the two immediately interrogated me concerning my origins and circumstances. Once again I repeated the old story, the tale of an orphan from Kiev seeking employment in the city, and I hoped that it would be accepted.

Maria was a beautiful woman with an elegant appearance and a peaches-and-cream complexion. Their home was full of handsome objects and elegant furniture. After a while I learned that this was booty plundered from the homes of the Jewish families in Babin and the surrounding area who had been sent to their deaths.

Petro was a thin man with a sparse blond mustache, thin lips and blue eyes. The master was in charge of all the cooking for the household because the pampered Maria never set foot in the kitchen. They had an old servant, a deaf-mute named Ivan, and an elderly maid named Marusya, a primitive gentile with no intellectual capacity whatsoever, who fed the pigs and milked the cows. Lucky for me, Marusya was preoccupied with her job and did not bother me.

I was given a job. My duties were to wake up early in the morning, before dawn, to prepare the flour for baking bread and to help with the cooking in the kitchen. Afterwards I had to take the six cows and their young calves to pasture and make sure they ate their fill of clover. I enjoyed spending time in the bosom of nature. I learned how to care for cattle, how to tie the cows' front legs so that they would not be able to run but rather would amble slowly in their section of the meadow. I wandered aimlessly for entire days, among the fields of wheat, grain and potatoes. The days passed pleasantly, and I was able to have a bit of relief from the horrors I had endured.

One day I woke up early as usual. However, I was extremely tired. A sense of unease had come over me during the night, and I had found it difficult to sleep. I was about to leave to pasture with the cows when Petro called me to the kitchen, saying he wished to speak to me. Filled with terror, I silently entered the kitchen. His blue eyes glinted like cold steel, and he hissed at me from between his thin lips. He looked me in the eyes and said to me, "You are a liar. Your story is false. You are a Jew! You were dreaming last night and you cried out, '*Mama, Mama, Mishlugt mir! Mehn hargeht mir! Helf mir!*' (Mother, Mother, they are beating me! They are killing me! Help me!)."

"I understand Yiddish," Petro went on in his cold voice. "I worked for Jews. Maria also knows because she heard you calling out in your sleep. You woke us up. We could not fall back asleep. You should know that Maria wishes to hand you over to the Gestapo. But I restrained her, God alone knows why," he said. Suddenly his tone seemed tender and soft. "I had compassion for you. In the spirit of Christianity, I have decided to let you live and raise you in the spirit of Christianity." I stared at him, dumbfounded. "You are a bright girl, a loyal servant," he continued. "You are different from the Jews whom I knew. You will help raise the child we are expecting, and I will convince Maria not to betray you to the Gestapo. In a few years we will marry you off to my younger brother, Boris."

I lowered my eyes. "We will not tell Boris now, nor my parents," he added. "Next Sunday you will meet them. We will prepare a magnificent feast for them, you and I."

Once again, God had taken pity on me. Once again my life had been handed to me like a gift. I had a roof over my head, a warm bed, a comfortable home and food to eat. Here in Maria and Petro's home, a new chapter in my life, a long and difficult one, had begun.

I learned to act in accordance with Maria's moods and to satisfy her every whim, but things did not always work out according to plan. One time Marusya became ill, and Maria instructed me to go to the barn to milk the cows in her place. I answered that I did not know how to milk them, and she replied, "Take a chair and a pitcher, and sit beside the cow. Begin pulling on her udders, and the milk will come out by itself." Barefoot, I waded through the manure in the barn which reached nearly to my knees. I sat on a small stool and began to milk. The cow, apparently, sensed an unfamiliar hand and kicked with her back leg. I became frightened, abandoned the pitcher and fled. Maria stood at the edge of the barn, observing me. "Go back and milk," she threatened me, beating me on my back and legs with a thin stick. I burst out in tears. "Be quiet, Jew," she commanded me. At the sound of screams and weeping, Petro came running to the barn. He commanded Maria to stop beating me. "I will take care of her," he said, and he approached me, calmed me down and explained how to

Family Portrait, 1937

Back row, from left: Chasya Bulba (Raizel's cousin); Shaya Rudiyak (Gershon and Chayka's son); Chayka Bulba (Gershon's wife); Gershon Rudiyak (husband of Aunt Chayka, Raizel's oldest sister); Gessya Bulba (Genya's aunt, Raizel's youngest sister); Itzik Bulba (Genya's uncle, brother of Raizel Bulba, Genya's mother).

Center row, from left: Rudya Bulba (Esther and Chaim's daughter, Grandfather Noah's sister); Esther Bulba (Grandfather Noah's wife, Genya's great-grandmother); Chaim Bulba (Grandfather Noah's father, Genya's great-grandfather); Noah Bulba (Genya's grandfather, Raizel's father).

Front row, from left: Genya Rudiyak (Chayka and Gershon's daughter); Genya Finkelstein; Chava Rudiyak (Chayka and Gershon's daughter).

Genya remembers going to the post office with her grandfather to mail this picture to her grandfather's brother, Asher Bulba, who lived then in Galveston, Texas.

This picture, and those on the following two pages, were taken out of Europe before the war and were later given to Genya by distant relatives.

Raizel Bulba, Genya's mother, 1934.

Itzik Bulba, Genya's uncle, Raizel's younger brother, 1928.

Moshe Bulba, Genya's uncle, Raizel's older brother, 1925.

At the training camp in Bernstein, Germany, 1946. Genya is with two Jewish partisans whom she met in Vienna: Willy (left) and Yomak (right).

OPPOSITE
TOP: A band composed of immigrant youths, Bernstein, Germany, 1946. Genya (standing next to the window) is the only female in the band.

BOTTOM: Genya (second from right) in Marseilles, before sailing to Israel, 1947.

General Mordechai (Moka) Limon, commander of the
illegal immigrant ship, November 29, 1947.

Genya (right) at the transit camp in Cyprus, 1947.
Her friend Vera sewed her shorts from sugar sacks.

Washday at the transit camp in Cyprus, 1947. Genya is second from left.

OPPOSITE
The family of Mordechai Schwartz-Tuvi, Genya's first husband, 1927.
Clockwise, from left: Mordechai, Chaya, Tovah (the mother), Peretz (the father),
Moishele, and Devorah.

LEFT
Mordechai Schwartz-Tuvi,
age 21, 1941.

BELOW
Genya (left) in Rehovot,
shortly before her
marriage, 1949.

Genya under the wedding canopy with
Mordechai Schwartz-Tuvi, Tel Aviv, 1949.

At Vered's bat mitzvah, 1962.
The last family portrait before Mordechai was killed in a work-related
accident. Genya is 32, Vered is 12, Tuvi is nearly 10.

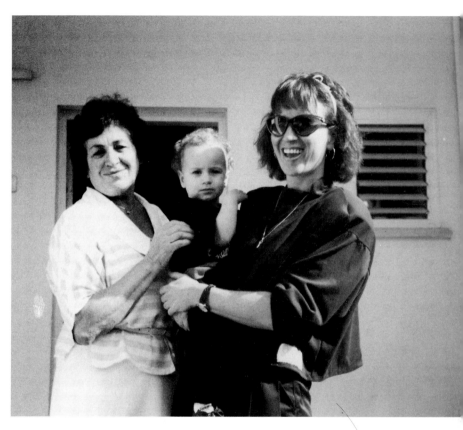

Genya with her daughter-in-law, Oli, and her granddaughter, Dana, 1987.

(Reproduced from Dr. Gerst Begel's Yiddish and Hebrew Yizkor book, *My Shtetl Berezna,* published in 1954 by Hamerkaz, Tel Aviv.)

This group of young people from Berezna returned there just after the end of World War II to create a memorial for the 3,000 Jews of Berezna who were murdered and buried in a common grave. The grave marker, made of wood, was erected at the site of the Berezna Jewish cemetery that had been destroyed by Ukrainians. The plaque on the monument reads:

HERE ARE BURIED 3,000 PEOPLE —

MEN, WOMEN AND CHILDREN —

KILLED ON THE 12TH OF ELUL

BY THE HITLERITE MURDERERS.

MAY THE MURDERERS' NAMES AND MEMORIES

BE FOREVER OBLITERATED.

The Russian inscription on the large monument above reads:

THE MEMORY OF THOSE WHO PERISHED
WILL ETERNALLY BE IN THE HEARTS OF THE PEOPLE OF BEREZNA.

Near the large monument, the Russian inscription on a common grave reads:

IN THIS PLACE, 25 OF AUGUST, 1942, FASCIST GERMAN
CONQUERORS EXECUTED 3,680 SOVIET CITIZENS.

Family Portrait, 1997

Back row, from left: Vered Tuvi-Yinon (Genya's daughter); Mickey Barzel (husband of Genya's granddaughter, Efrat); Gaby Yinon; Oren (Vered's son; Genya's grandson); Eli Zeltzer (Genya's second husband)

Front row, from left: Efrat (Genya's granddaugher) holding her son, Ben; Genya holding her great-granddaughter, Maya; Tuvi (Genya's son); Ori (Tuvi's son; Genya's grandson).

milk a cow. "You will succeed," he said, "because you have a very strong will."

I resumed milking. Petro stood on the side to supervise me. "This is how a young Ukrainian girl works," he praised me. Afterwards he changed his mind. "This work is too hard for a young girl," he said suddenly and took over the milking himself.

"Try to smile at Maria," the master advised me. "Even if she beats you, don't show her that you are angry. Speak to her with respect." I acted according to his advice. I addressed her as "*Panny Maria*," Mistress Maria, because she was the granddaughter of a Polish squire and acted like a princess. With time our relationship improved, and she began to like me so much that I became her personal maid. Sometimes in rare moments of kindness, she would give me her old dresses to wear when I went to church on Sunday.

I was lonely. I lived in a home with two adults. We had no mutual topics of conversation. Sometimes on Sundays, my day off, Stefa would invite me for lunch in her home. Her family was well-off, and they were reputed to be fanatic Jew-haters. Once Stefa told me that they had hidden a Jewish family in their home in exchange for a great deal of money and gold jewelry. But after a while her father had gone to the Germans and informed them about the Jews in hiding. The Germans arrived toward morning, accompanied by the Ukrainian militia, and took the entire Jewish family, even the little children, to a field not far from the house, where they murdered them. I was stunned by the casualness with which Stefa described the extermination of an entire family. Stefa, however, interpreted my behavior differently. In her naiveté, she thought that I too wanted to see firsthand the site of the murders, and she took me to the hill where they had buried the slain Jews. I had no choice but to follow her as if in a drugged stupor. She showed me the place, and then we returned to her house. That day at lunch, I was unable to eat even one bite. I didn't know that Jewish family, but the echoes of the shots resounded in my ears. I could not stop thinking about the murder of my beloved family. The picture of my mother pleading for our lives was constantly before my eyes.

Afterwards Stefa escorted me home. I locked myself in my small room and was unable to get out of bed. Maria and Petro inquired about my health. I told them that apparently I had an upset stomach. The next few days were very difficult for me. I had to carry on with my work without arousing anyone's suspicion, especially not Stefa's and her family's, but I was seized with a terrible weakness and found it difficult even to stand and complete my work.

Maria's disdainful attitude toward me got worse. I received insults and curses at every step. The thin stick she used to beat me with never left her hand. I remember one Sunday morning. I was getting ready to go to church. Maria called me to come to her, and with the ruler in her hand she separated sections of my thick hair. "Lice inspection," she announced. She continued the inspection while I trembled in fear.

Suddenly she yelled, "Where are the big scissors?"

"In the storage shed," I stuttered.

I brought her the scissors. She pulled me to her roughly and said, "Sit here, outside. Quick! And not a word!" And with a swipe of her hand Maria cut off my two beautiful braids. She wasn't satisfied with cutting my braids but continued, as one possessed, pulling clumps of my hair and hacking them off brutally and wildly, until I was left nearly bald.

My heart broke from shame and pain. "Mistress Maria," I said to her, wailing, "I washed my hair with a lot of soap. I poured kerosene on it more than once. I do not have lice or even nits. Why have you done this to me?"

"Lice or no lice," she answered with growing apathy, while pushing me into the house so the neighbors should not see me crying, "now your hair will grow in again, and it will not be the hair of a stinking Jew."

I was very miserable. "What shall I tell my friends in the church," I thought, "about what has happened to my hair?"

Stefa came to visit me, and she was shocked by my "new look." Unlike me, she was wearing a fancy dress, and her two blond braids had ribbons. I was very jealous of her, and I remembered my mother combing my hair so tenderly, with so much love. I remembered how she would weave colorful ribbons into my braids and finish off with a kiss on my forehead. I could not control my tears. Stefa could not find words with which to comfort me and ran home quickly. It seemed to me that I saw tears glistening in her eyes.

Maria locked me in the servants' kitchenette and said to me, "You deserve to be punished. Why did you cry in front of your friend?"

"Mistress Maria," I replied, "the tears flowed by themselves."

"As punishment you will not receive any food until

the evening," she said. And she whipped me on the legs and back with her stick. "In the evening, you will go to Stefa and tell her I was forced to cut your hair because you had cuts on your head. I am saving you from certain death by not revealing your secret. Instead of whining you should be thanking me. I am warning you, do not tell Master Petro about the blows you received from me. Do you hear?"

I was very hungry on that accursed Sunday. Toward evening Maria ordered me to feed the pigs, the calves and the horses. "Marusya and Ivan have not returned from their day off," Maria said. "Finish all the chores and sit down to eat."

The summer was at its peak. In the garden and the forest there was a lot of fruit. Maria used to send me to pick the fruits, to wash them and to prepare jam from them. We cooked the fruit in a large pot in the yard according to Mother's recipe, and when the mixture cooled we poured the jam into small glass jars, which we covered with muslin. In a short time I became expert at making these preserves, and Maria told her husband proudly that I learned quickly and that the previous maid, who had been much older than I, had never been as good.

Once my cooking skills were known, Petro decided that I would help him with the cooking and they would hire another maid to tend the pigs. Every morning we would gather vegetables from the garden to prepare the day's meals. Often guests at their home would include German officers who lived in Babin and were in charge of the sugar factory, as well as Ukrainians, Petro's friends in the underground. The leader of the underground was Stefan Bandera, the son of a Galician priest. He led a group that was fighting for Ukrainian independence. The *Bandrovitsim*, as they were nicknamed, assisted the Germans with killing the Jews, especially in the villages and forest, places that the *Bandrovitsim* knew so well. In exchange for these murderous deeds, the Germans promised them a country of their own. Stefan Bandera was later killed in Russia by Russian soldiers.

On the weekends we would prepare an assortment of delicacies for the festive noontime meal on Sundays. The Germans, the village priest and other important people enjoyed these dinners very much. Before the guests arrived I would leave the house so that the Ukrainians would not identify me, and in the evening Petro would come with the wagon to pick me up from Stefa's house or Tanya's. Tanya was a new Ukrainian friend I had met through Maria. Tanya's family lived a short distance from Maria and Petro's farm, and I became very friendly with her when we sang together in the church choir. Her two brothers, of course, served in the Ukrainian militia, and more than once I heard talk in their home about the murder of Jews who had been hiding in the area. They boasted of these deeds and said that soon the area would finally be rid of Jews. They specialized, according to what they said, in "swift and efficient" treatment.

I was only thirteen years old, but I had learned how to suppress the ache deep inside me. Since I wanted to survive, I took care to conceal my emotions, and I needed to draw upon great reserves of spiritual strength. I learned to play my role, to laugh with them, to share their gaiety. More than once in Maria and Petro's home I saw silver candlesticks and silver wine goblets with the words "Kosher for Passover" and a beautiful tablecloth embroidered with Hebrew lettering. But I never asked where those items came from. My heart would contract within me, and I would remain silent. Those silver utensils reminded me of my home and my childhood so long ago, now gone forever— never, I knew, to return. I thought it had been decreed that I remain a maid in Maria's home for the rest of my life.

Once my friend Tanya's mother asked me where I came from, and what my life had been like. Once more I repeated the familiar tale. She looked at me and said, as they all did, "Genya, you have Jewish eyes." I burst out laughing. "My mother was Ukrainian. Her name was Katya Stepaniyuk." I repeated the story for the umpteenth time. "And my father was an Uzbeki or a Gruzini." I was seized by fear that they would tell on me and betray me to the Germans.

Workers from neighboring farms came to help out with harvesting the potatoes on Maria and Petro's farm just as we, the farm laborers, went to help out at nearby farms when necessary. Once when I was at a neighboring farm, a young mare kicked me. I collapsed and lost consciousness. When I awoke I found myself in bed in my room. My head hurt, and I was very dizzy. Apparently I had suffered a concussion. I worried that while unconscious, once again, I might have blurted out words in Yiddish. Maria was very angry and ill-tempered, and I didn't know why. I figured that it was hard for her to manage without me. She would yell at me a lot and beat me without mercy with her thin stick. During this period the Germans were more frequent visitors, and I had to rise extra early to prepare their meals. Petro also prepared distilled vodka for them from potatoes and grain, which fermented for several days. The entire day, until late in the evening, the vodka would drip through a thin tube into a huge bottle, and I would have to check that the liquor did not drain out anywhere else.

Another difficult winter began with storms, blizzards and torrential rains. During the storms many chickens, pigs and calves were swept away and drowned. Stefa's parents, our Czech neighbors, came to help us, and we worked day and night, clearing away the erosion that changed the path of the stream and caused the flooding. Together with these good neighbors, we overcame the problems that nature placed in our path. Nevertheless, severe blizzards continued to plague the farm, and we worked daily, soaked and exhausted, to maintain the structures and the barns.

Shortly after I came to live at Maria's, I realized that she had a lover. He was a Ukrainian fellow, tall and handsome, named Ivan, an officer in the German army, serving in the forests near Rovna. He pursued her with great ardor and came to visit with many gifts. When he was on duty and could not come to the farm, he would send her love letters. Maria did not know where to hide all these letters. Finally she gave them to me to hide beneath my mattress, and I became a partner to the lovers' secret. However, the romance ended when Ivan was transferred to the center of Poland.

Within a short time Maria became friendly with another German officer, one of the regular guests in her home. Shamelessly she recounted to me acts of slaughter "her" officer had carried out against the Jews of the Rovna ghetto. I would breathe deeply and try to hide the flood of emotions that these stories aroused in me. Maria was very moody. At times she was easy-going and light-hearted, and suddenly, without warning, she would resume beating me. I received brutal blows for the smallest infraction. I learned to stay as far away from her as possible on the bad days. I did my work, especially tending her son, Tarras, whom I raised with much love, which he returned. Sometimes it seemed that Maria was jealous of the loving bond we shared, but we never discussed this.

Petro was involved in the underground and was absent from the farm for long periods of time. Rumors flew in the village that the Germans were looking for him and that a monetary reward was guaranteed to anyone who would hand him over, dead or alive. From snatches of conversation between Maria and Petro's father I learned that Petro had caused the death of many of his German guests. Petro and his comrades in the Bandera gang would murder the Germans when they returned, drunk from their evening amusements, on their way to their main headquarters in the city of Rovna.

One Sunday guests from the local area gathered at the house. They were still sitting around the table, full of all sorts of delicacies, and eating, when one of the young gentile women looked my way and suddenly called out, "This is a Jew!"

My blood froze in my veins. A great tumult arose at the table. Petro sizzled with rage. How had he not realized that someone might identify me? At first the guests did not believe what the young girl was saying, but she insisted she was sure because during the Polish regime she had worked for my Aunt Sheindel in Ostra. This time I was certain that I had been identified and that my end was near. My consciousness receded; I nearly fainted, but Petro and his younger brother made light of her words. Petro called her outside. "You are drunk!" he told her, and he convinced her that she was wrong and had confused me with someone else. He yelled at her for having ruined the festive mood and told his friends that he had known my deceased mother, who had been, according to him, "a pure Ukrainian." I was restless all night. Filled with terror, I prayed in my bed.

Because the neighbors would report one another, the Germans would frequently conduct raids on individual homes in their search for Jews in hiding. One day the Germans surrounded Maria and Petro's farm and the farm where my Czech friend, Stefa, lived. Ukrainians from the neighboring village, Novoselki, had reported that Jews had escaped to the area of our farm. The Germans came and searched, assisted by their dogs, turning the granary upside down, combing the barn and everywhere else, but they found no Jews.

The winter days passed slowly, with hard work and constant fear: fear of the Germans, of the weather, of the unknown. One cold winter day a woman, no longer young, came to the farm dressed in faded and torn clothing. She appeared weak and hungry. I took pity on her and gave her a bit of food, a lump of lard, bread and cheese. I told her, in Ukrainian of course, that she should get out of here quickly and go to another area because here they are always searching for Jews. She told me that she was from a village near Rovna, and her two children were wandering about, hungry, in the neighboring village. It did not seem that she understood my warning. With a surprising glance, she thanked me for the food I had given her. I realized that the instinct for survival is stronger than all feelings of fear and danger. I pleaded with her to leave. I suggested that she pose as a gypsy, with her dark hair. Much later, when the war had ended, I met her by chance in the city of Rovna, when she was on her way to Israel.

Maria's German lover would bring many gifts: bottles of perfume, silk lingerie and also gold jewelry and diamonds, plundered from the homes of Jews who had been sent to the death camps. Maria adored these presents. She would allow only me to launder her expensive silk slips, and I did this with the greatest care and attention to detail. She asked me to polish the jewelry thoroughly with a brush and soap and water in order to remove what she claimed was "Jewish sweat" that was still stuck to them.

Since I was performing all the household chores, including caring for the child and the laundry, Maria had a great deal of free time during the day to dress and beautify herself. She wore elegant dresses and appeared absolutely gorgeous all the time. Things were going well for me in those days. Maria did not beat me, and she even complimented my baking. She would brag to her guests about what a wonderful baker her maid, Genya, was. I baked poppyseed cakes and cakes filled with dried fruits; I tried to cook and bake like Mother, and I succeeded. Her German officer was also pleased with her faithful maid. I did everything for him. I cooked for him, washed his socks and shined his shoes. He spoke to me in Ukrainian mixed with German, and I would nod my head as if I understood German. In the morning I would churn fresh butter for him, which he would spread in thick layers on slices of the bread that I had baked.

After a while the German officer's wife learned of the affair between Maria and her husband, and one clear morning she appeared at our door, a tall German with a freckled face, clutching their young son in her arms and accompanied by a female Ukrainian translator. Without the slightest twinge of fear or hesitation, I answered that I took care of Maria and Petro's son and earned my keep cooking, doing laundry and performing various tasks, and that I had never seen her husband.

Maria was beside herself. Filled with emotion, she thanked me for my firm stance under the interrogation, for I had not displayed the slightest sign of fear, answering all the German woman's questions confidently without betraying the lovers' secret.

That winter was especially long and difficult. Because of the fierce cold, I suffered severe pains in the joints of my leg. I also suffered bladder problems from the days when I had gone barefoot in the forests. But I did not lack warm clothing and sturdy boots. Maria gave me her large wardrobe of used clothing, and I could choose for myself any article of clothing that she had discarded after only one or two wearings.

Finally the winter passed, and toward spring there was a great deal of work in the field. Maria and I drafted Ukrainian and Polish workers from among the area residents. Petro's father came to our aid. He and his wife moved in with us, into their daughter-in-law's home. The father helped out with the farm work, and Petro's mother helped in the kitchen with great energy. She was most appreciative of my help to the family, and she praised me to her husband. Many times she said that she would like me to become her daughter-in-law, and that when the time came I should marry her son Boris, Petro's younger brother. In the evenings we would sit together to sew and embroider. I embroidered a beautiful tablecloth for her in the custom of Ukrainian brides who prepare gifts for their future "parents." We even wove the cloth ourselves. In the summer we picked the cotton, and then we wove white cloth that was smooth and pleasant next to the skin. From the cloth we also made linens, towels, tablecloths and even embroidered dresses. I learned all these skills from my friends, and especially from my friend Stefa and her mother. The dresses were so lovely that even the German officer, Maria's lover, ordered one for his daughter. Her measurements were similar to mine, so we did not need to measure her for the dress.

Maria loved to embroider and taught me this delicate craft. Precision was most important to her, and she would not tolerate any mistakes. I received blows from her for any mistakes I made in the cross-stitching, but I controlled myself and remained silent. I knew that Maria was nervous and on edge because now that Petro's aged parents had come to live with us, it was difficult for her to arrange trysts with her lover. When the old ones would go to sleep, the lovers would rendezvous in the guest room on the lower level of the house. I would guard the dogs so that they would not bark when the German officer arrived. The next morning, the officer's driver would arrive to return him to headquarters. On those mornings Maria was very sweet to me, loving and generous, and those days would go by without shouting or blows.

One night Petro came to visit his son and his wife. Maria was not at home. She had gone on a trip to Rovna with her lover. Indeed, she had left me with instructions for running the household, but she had not told me how to act with her husband if he came for a visit.

I awoke from my sleep to the sound of Petro's yelling as he searched for his wife. "Damn it," he shouted. "Where is Maria?" "She has gone to Rovna to buy Easter clothes," I said. "And probably she slept over at her friend, Sonia's." Her friend worked at the Nazi headquarters and lived in Rovna.

Petro drank himself into a stupor and went to sleep at one of his friends'. He feared sleeping overnight in his own house because he knew the Germans were looking for him all over the region. The next day was full of tension for me. Maria returned in the evening, all smiles and joy, the fragrance of her beautiful perfume filling the house. I told her about Petro's visit. She turned pale, but when she heard my story she calmed down and showered me with love and affection and thanked me for lying for her.

At the end of that summer, shots were heard in the

area of the farm. The Czech neighbors told Maria that the Russians were advancing. The Germans had begun to prepare for a retreat. They burned documents and files and went wild in the sugar factory, tossing sacks of sugar around as if they were sand. The main road became clogged with retreating soldiers, but I was not even happy about their defeat. I couldn't even think about running away because I remembered Petro's threat that if I ever left him or told about his past he would follow me all the days of my life to the ends of the earth until he found me and killed me.

In the suburbs of Babin a Jewish family was hiding in a trench they had dug near Novoselki when they escaped from the ghetto. One day I found them hiding in an abandoned building that belonged to Maria's parents. There was a young girl among them; she was beautiful, with fair hair and a gentile appearance. Every morning, risking her life, she would go to seek work in the area, and in the evening she would return with a bit of food for the family to eat.

I discovered them by chance. One day I went out to search for one of the cows, which had gotten lost in the thick shrubs, and I happened upon one of the children, who had left the bunker to bring water from a small waterfall in the area. When he saw me he became very frightened. He looked pitiful; his torn clothing and hat made me feel sorry for him and reminded me of my little brothers, who had been killed. Then I saw a woman near him. She looked at me in a pitiful way and asked if I had some bread. The boy mumbled a few words in Yiddish. I immediately realized that she was a Jew. Weeping, she begged me not to tell that I had found their hiding place. I promised to keep her secret on the condition that she would not tell anyone if I helped her.

I returned home, full of emotions, and I found it difficult to carry out my routine household chores. The next morning, when I went to the pasture with the cows, I secretly took some food with me. I also wrapped and took an old outfit of Petro's and one of my own that was too big for me. I went to the place where I had met them and gave them the package. The boy, who reminded me of Leibele, hungrily swallowed the cheese and yogurt I had brought. Pictures of my own beloved family filled my mind and came before my eyes. I stayed with them a few moments and promised to return. Every two or three days I would go there, bringing a bit of food. One day I could not find them. I searched the area but found no trace of them. Later I learned that a local farmer had seen them and betrayed them to the Germans. They murdered all of them.

I went through difficult days. I could not stop thinking about them, especially the little boy who reminded me so much of my brother and for whom I had risked my life by bringing him a bit of food. In my heart, I thanked G-d that no one had seen me coming or going while visiting them. Otherwise, my fate would have been the same as theirs.

Toward the end of the war, a rift developed between the Germans and the Ukrainians. The Ukrainians wanted their own independent country, and Petro and the other members of Stefan Bandera's group began killing the Germans to avenge that broken promise. Petro's friends told him about Maria's affair with the German officer and about her frequent trips to Rovna, and he began to keep an eye on her.

One morning men of the Gestapo surrounded the house. Maria was not home, and I was frightened to death. I held Tarras tightly and pressed him to my heart. They came, accompanied by dogs, and it was clear that they were looking for Bandera's people. Two German natives who had lived in the Ukraine for many years interrogated me in Ukrainian and asked if the German officer, Egun, had slept over recently. I answered that I had seen no one, that I slept alone with the child in his room, and that the old servants and the laborers slept in the other rooms. One of the Germans put his gun to my head and demanded to know, "Tell me, girl. Have you heard shots nearby?" "I swear, sir," I said, quick to genuflect, "I have heard no shots, nor have I seen the German officer." I was pale because I knew that Petro had killed the German officer and several of his comrades not far from our home.

One day during the last summer that the Germans remained on Ukrainian soil, Maria said to me that she was going "to help out Bandera's youths." She said she was also going to search for her mother's family.

She left, and I stayed at home to care for young Tarras. It soon became clear that, fearing the Russians, Maria had left us and fled with her husband. Petro, like all of the men in Bandera's group, had taken part in the murder of many Russian and Jewish partisans. Without the assistance of Ukrainians like Petro and his comrades, the Germans would never have been able to have such an easy time exterminating the many Jews who had sought refuge in the forests. They had betrayed the Jews to the Germans in exchange for rewards. They took part in the murder of my parents and brothers and my entire large family so that no one remained except me. They had murdered those who escaped from the camps, the death trains, the ghettos and the bunkers.

The Germans persisted in checking the farm frequently and interrogating us as to the whereabouts of its owners. I told them that the couple had left in anger, the husband setting out for parts unknown, vowing to me that he would never return, and the wife had gone off separately, and we had no idea where she had gone.

After a while the Germans' pressure on the local townsfolk let up, maybe because they changed their headquarters to a different area. This gave Maria and Petro the opportunity to return home. Little by little life returned to normal, and Petro resumed his old habit of disappearing from time to time for several days at a stretch.

At the end of the summer of 1944 I left Maria and Petro's home, intending never to come back. This is what happened. Thoughts of my Jewishness preyed on my mind constantly. I longed to return to the city, thinking that maybe I would find a survivor from my family, but I feared Petro. Finally one day I had my chance. Petro came home for a brief rest and was surprised to see that no one was home. He asked me where his wife was.

"Maria has gone with the servant, Ivan, to the cemetery to lay flowers on her parents' graves," I answered.

"Harness the mare to the wagon at once," he said impatiently. "Take Tarras with you and ride quickly to the cemetery. Tell the mistress to return at once since I have come for only a short while." As I harnessed the mare a thought occurred to me.

"Tarras is a small boy," I said. "He is liable to fall out of the wagon. Maybe he should remain at home. I will return immediately." Petro didn't answer, and I understood his silence to be agreement with my suggestion.

I harnessed the mare to the wagon and went alone to the cemetery. Everything was very quiet. A light breeze ruffled the treetops, and the song of a single bird broke the silence. I tied the horse to the fence at the side of the road and began walking quickly toward the highway. I walked a long way. I hoped to reach the village of Hoshts. I remembered that we had had family there, Aunt Paula, her husband and children, and other cousins of Father. I trudged along for hours. On the way I met a farmer, his wagon hitched to a team of horses. I stopped and greeted him. He asked me where I was going. I told him I hoped to go to Hoshts. "My aunt teaches in the school there," I said, "and I am on my way to her, but since it is growing late I am looking for a place to sleep."

The wagon driver scrutinized my face with steady eyes and answered that I was welcome to come and sleep in his home. I accepted the invitation gratefully and climbed on his wagon. On the way he told me that a few Jews had returned to Hoshts. "What a pity they didn't kill them all," he said. I agreed with a heavy heart. When we reached his home I met his family. He had four children, among them a girl exactly my age. After the evening meal they suggested that I remain with them for a while because they needed more hands to help with the harvest. I thanked them for the offer but explained that I was on my way to Hoshts, to my aunt, a teacher of Ukrainian language, and on my way back to Babin I would return to visit them.

Early in the morning I went on my way. On the road I saw convoys of Russian soldiers and many vehicles. After walking for many hours, I became tired and stretched out my hand to hitch a ride, but not one car stopped for me. I walked on for a long time, and finally a car stopped. Two women were inside, one of them a Jewish doctor and the other a Russian soldier. They had the Red Cross insignia and military medical tags. The doctor tried to speak to me in Yiddish. I told them that I did not have the strength to walk anymore, that I was a Jew and that I wanted to reach Hoshts. They spoke in Russian, and I answered in Ukrainian. For the first time since that dreadful night I told the true story. I told how we had lived in the forests, how my entire family had been killed and how I had survived the war years. They said it seemed that very few Jews were still in the area, but they promised to direct me to the survivors when we reached the city.

We reached Hoshts. I wandered about the Jewish area for hours. Suddenly I saw candles burning in one of the windows and realized that it was Sabbath eve. I approached the house and knocked on the door. A woman with a scarf on her head opened the door, looked at me and asked what I wanted. I tried to answer in Yiddish, but I couldn't produce a sound. Immediately I pulled myself together and told her in Ukrainian that I was a Jew, the daughter of Wolf and Raizel Finkelstein. The woman recognized me and, with much emotion, reminded me that she and her family had visited my Grandfather in his village several years ago. She said that she remembered my parents and brothers. She, her husband—a tailor—and four children had managed to stay alive. They were lucky because they had joined the partisans in the Zhitomir region. I asked if she knew my father's cousins Yantel and Pessya Finkelstein and their children, and I learned that they had been killed by the Ukrainians.

I remained in the tailor's home. The wife tried to support the family with odd jobs, and she put me in charge of all the housework. Once again I found myself cooking and doing the laundry. The master of the house would roam through the area's villages, and with great difficulty he eked out a living as a tailor. The children were already grown, which made things much easier for them.

Several years later I learned that before his death, Labku, the mayor of the village of Kolesniki, charged his sons with the duty of caring for the cherry orchard and the graves of Grandfather Noah and Grandmother Esther. After the war when I was in Hoshts, I wanted to see that place again. My friends warned me to stay out of the villages because the locals hated Jews. "You will return wrapped in a blanket," they said to me, "as a corpse." Later I heard that from time to time someone had been placing flowers in the cherry orchard. I am sure that it was Labku and his good wife and their son, Padusio. The villagers destroyed Grandfather's house and tore out all the door posts and doors. They had decided to eradicate all traces of our family. I was frightened that if I showed my face in the village Bandera's men might try to kill me, too, so that no remnant at all of the family would be left.

For many years I dreamed about Grandfather's house and his cherry orchard, the dahlias and the hollyhocks that grew in the garden. To this day in my dreams I climb the mound of earth, Grandfather Noah and Grandmother Esther's grave, or the cherry and apple trees. The pain follows me even in my dreams. In my mind's eye I see my whole family gathered there, Mother in a white dress and high-heeled shoes, and I in a fancy dress with red and white ribbons braided into my hair. I am standing on a chair and reciting a poem about Pilsudski, Poland's premier. I am reciting and accompanying my words with emphatic hand motions about "our" Poland with a star shining above it. Mother comes over and hugs me. And her Polish friends applaud loudly. Aunt Chayka cries, overcome with emotion, and childless Uncle Itzik, who had loved me more than all of them, hugs me and presses me to his heart.

Grandfather Noah Bulba and his wife Rachel were also caught and killed. Even rich Aunt Sheindel was not spared the brutal death that the Germans had decreed for us. She was murdered along with her children in the Ostra ghetto. The Germans had killed her husband earlier, after robbing him of all the family's gold. Aunt Bayla, her sandy-haired husband and all the members of her family died in the Rovna ghetto. That is how it was with all of them, every last one.

six

I Remain Alive

In Hoshts I met Adik, a charming fellow. His parents had perished, and he was living with relatives near the tailor's home. The first time I saw him he was dressed in the uniform of a Russian soldier. He stared at me and asked, "Who is this little beauty?" The tailor's wife repeated for him as briefly as possible the story of my escape from Maria and Petro. His eyes gleamed. In those days he and his friends were hunting down members of Stefan Bandera's group. I told him the story of my life, how I had lived as a Christian with a Ukrainian family and that I wanted to continue my education but feared going into the city. Adik was armed with a rifle, and he offered to accompany me to school. In the evenings he would come to visit me, and once he brought me a beautiful silk scarf that had belonged to his dead mother, a keepsake his aunt had given him after his mother died. "See how it suits your hair," he said. Sometimes he would bring me Russian chocolate. "I saw you a while ago," he said, "but didn't dare approach." He told me that he admired my intelligence, which had kept me alive, and felt instinctively that I was looking for someone with whom to share the horrors I had experienced. He said that when I grew up I would understand the bond of warmth and love that we shared. I told him that I intended to leave Hoshts and travel to Berezna to search for a relative, any relative from my large family who might have remained alive. I told him I was afraid of the Ukrainian thugs, and he said, "You will not travel alone. The roads are dangerous and full of murderers. Now you are in my care, and I will guard you." He promised to take me to Berezna in two weeks when he returned from military duty.

I loved Adik. He filled me with a sense of warmth and security. He filled an emotional hollow deep within me, an emptiness that I thought would never be filled again.

At the tailor's house I met a good-hearted woman who had lost her children in the Holocaust. She suggested that I move into her home and enroll in the government school in Hoshts. I accepted her generous offer. She took care of me with great warmth and encouraged me to concentrate on my schoolwork. Indeed, within a very short time I became an excellent student. After years during which I had not even held a book, notebook or pen in my hands, I was thrilled to restart my education, and I put my entire being into my studies. In that way, at least for a little while, I was able to forget the horrors that had been my constant companions for so long.

One day on my way home from school, I saw a crowd in the street. People stood around weeping. A woman who recognized me tried to lead me away from there. "What happened?" I asked her. "They have murdered Adik," she responded. My eyes clouded over. Once again my world had collapsed around me.

The next day Adik was buried among the ruins of the

Jewish cemetery of Hoshts. A handful of Jews gathered there, the last remnants of Jewry, and we cut a path through the narrow roads, overgrown with weeds. A few men carried Adik's corpse, wrapped in a blanket stained with blood. Russian soldiers stood by, guarding us from Bandera's men. The funeral was heart-rending and terrifying; with no cantor, no eulogy and no honor, the corpse was lowered into the earth.

The harrowing memories of the funeral gave me no peace. Once again I could not sleep at night. My studies gradually became a burden. My wounded soul was dashed to smithereens. I thought of Adik constantly. A young flower, the sole survivor of his family, who had courageously and steadily persisted in fighting the Ukrainian murderers, had been cut down in the prime of life.

One day in the corridor at school I happened to run into Stefa, my Czech friend from Babin. She was in the class above me. Our meeting was emotional. She called, "Genya!" and I called back, "Stefa!" We remained locked in an embrace for several long moments. I told her the truth I had concealed from her all those years, that I was Jewish. She told me that after my disappearance Petro and his friends had searched the entire area for me. Petro thought that perhaps wild beasts had attacked me. He could not believe that I would leave them because I had always said that I was happy with them. I begged Stefa not to mention me to Maria and Petro. I wanted them to leave me in peace. "I am a Jew, and I want to live among Jews," I said to her.

After meeting Stefa, fear of Petro took over my life. I was afraid that he would come one day to take me back to the farm. Terror and my memories of Adik haunted me, and I decided, "I am going to go to Berezna, and what will be will be." True, I was living with a kind and good woman, but I yearned to make contact with someone from my own family.

There was no regular transportation between Hoshts and Berezna, so I made my way to the main road. Many Red Army military trucks filled with food and supplies passed me by, going toward Berezna. I stood by the road the entire day, and no one stopped for me. Finally an older soldier, driving a truck, stopped. Another soldier and a young girl sat beside him. He apologized that he had no room up front, but he offered to let me ride in the back of the truck. I stretched out comfortably among the sacks of vegetables and made holes in a few of the sacks so I could eat a few carrots and stalks of kohlrabi. I traveled, munching the juicy vegetables with gusto.

When we reached the city of Kostopol the soldier said, "Girl, get off here." I went to the train station in Kostopol. I found it in ruins from the bombings and very neglected. The platform was full of people; packages and bags of all sorts were strewn about. Despite having eaten the Red Army's vegetables, I was ravenous. I did not have a penny in my pocket, much less a ruble with which to purchase a train ticket.

The hours passed. The sun set, and night fell. I fell asleep among the packages waiting to be loaded on the freight train. I awoke early in the morning. There was lot of noise, and people milled all around. Now I was so hungry that I was actually dizzy. On the platform, not far from me, there was a family sitting on top of their packages, eating. At the sight of people eating so heartily I nearly went out of my mind. I decided to approach them. When they sensed my presence, they greeted me and asked where I was going. I was afraid to tell them that I was a Jew. I said that I was a Ukrainian from Kiev, on my way to Berezna to look for work.

When they saw me staring at their food, they took pity on me and suggested that I join them. One of the children held out a pita-like flatbread spread with fat and garlic. I fell upon the pita and swallowed it so quickly that I nearly choked. I finished up with half a bottle of water. Afterwards I felt better. I left, thanking them, and continued waiting, without any way to buy a ticket for the train. While I waited I became friendly with a Ukrainian girl who, like me, was penniless. Suddenly the train appeared and pulled into the station. "Here is the train! Climb aboard!" the girl urged me. I felt too weak and was sure that I could not manage to board the train when it started moving. She jumped onto the slow-moving train, held out her hand to me and shouted in Ukrainian, "Get on already." With my last bit of strength, I ran after the moving train, my arms outstretched, and with her strong arms she pulled me into the railroad car.

Finally I arrived in Berezna, where I began searching for survivors from my family. I was told that very few remained from the families who had been hiding in the forests. From the entire Bulba family—the uncles, aunts, cousins, grandfathers, grandmothers—no one had been spared. One woman I had known, named Sonia, told me that they were all buried in a mass grave outside the city. "The Germans and Ukrainians killed them all," she told me. I was also appalled at the appearance of the village itself. Homes that I had known had completely disappeared. No flowers or trees remained. The garden surrounding the church had been destroyed, as had the school on Komisarska Street. On the bread line, I met a pleasant man named Pinya Chobers. He asked, "Who are you, girl?" "Genya Finkelstein," I answered him, "the daughter of Raizel and the granddaughter of Noah Bulba." It seemed he had known my family. "How were you spared?" he asked, stunned, looking with compassion at my torn cloth shoes. I told him everything that had happened to me since leaving Berezna. "Who are you looking for here?" he asked. I listed the family members whom I still hoped to find among the ruins of the village.

He told me that all of them, to the last, had perished. When he saw how distraught I was he took pity on me and said, "There, in that house with a porch, lives Edka Rudiyak, who works as a midwife in the hospital. She is a distant relative of yours." I remembered her and that she had gone to complete her education in Warsaw. He told me that her husband had been killed in the forests and that she, along with her daughter, had survived.

Edka greeted me joyfully, and I moved in with her. However, it soon became clear that once again I had become a maid. While Edka went to work in the hospital, she expected me to prepare lunch for her daughter so that it would be ready when she returned from school. Also, I had to purchase the geese, pluck their feathers and cook them.

And she complained about the amount of butter I spread on my bread. I used a lot of butter because I loved it so much.

I was terrified at the thought that I would never find a place for myself in the world. "Will I never again be happy? Was it my lot to know only despair and sorrow?" I missed the days in Hoshts. There I had gone to school and had had Adik to lean on. I prayed for death. I wanted to drown myself in the river.

One day I met Yonik Sapoznik in the street; he was a young man I had known before the war. "You look familiar, girl," he said. "Aren't you a cousin of Genya Rudiyak?" "Yes," I answered sadly. "Why are you so gloomy?" he asked. He lived with his mother and his brother and invited me to his home for a meal. After so many years of wandering, I again saw a home filled with warmth. I noticed how his mother cooked the meal with care, how she set the table and served us. True, Yonik's father had been killed in the forests, but at least he had a mother. I envied him. "I have no home and no mother," I burst out in tears. I explained to them that I was alone in the world and did not know where to turn. They told me about two kind, childless women, Manya Zlotnik and Kayla Bayzman, who lived nearby. They promised to introduce me to them in the hope that perhaps one of them would adopt me as a daughter.

And, indeed, that is what happened. Manya, it seemed, was impressed with me, and shortly after we met she adopted me, and I became her daughter.

Manya provided me with a warm and loving home.

Once again I returned to school. I loved learning and again proved to be an excellent student. Manya and Kayla's husbands were serving, at the time, in the Russian Army. The two of them, therefore, found it convenient to live together. Manya was not fluent in Russian and asked me to write a letter to her husband, Chaim, to tell him that she had adopted an orphan. I remember very clearly how proud she was of that letter.

seven

Journeys

Chaim returned home, and we decided to relocate to Israel. We started out on the long trip, stopping temporarily in the city of Bytom, in the Polish heartland. There we were joined by Kayla Bayzman and her husband, Hershel. In Bytom there was a Jewish community center for refugees. The Jewish community, with the assistance of J.O.I.N.T., helped out the few who had managed to survive the Holocaust. The Center gave us an apartment, free of charge. It had been the apartment of a German who had fled during the war, and we settled in there.

My "parents" registered me as their daughter on their identification certificate, and I received the new name "Genya Zlotnik." They shared the food packages I received from J.O.I.N.T. They were also not shy about sharing with gusto the packages Grandfather's brother, Asher Bulba, sent me from Texas after he found me through the efforts of the Red Cross.

Within a short time I found that once again I had taken over the chore of caring for my new family. The Zlotniks supposedly had adopted me to be a daughter to them, but in truth they merely wanted to use me to change their money on the black market. This was illegal. Nevertheless, they trusted fate and hoped also that if I were caught I would not be punished because of my age.

They gave me Polish money, *zlotys*, and I changed it on the black market for German marks. I was always afraid that the Polish police were on my trail. Meanwhile, Manya and Chaim made a profit from these exchanges. This was the way I earned my keep while I was with them.

Afterwards, I joined a youth group, Hashomer Hatsa'ir (The Young Guard), but when my comrades went to Israel to the kibbutz, Ayn Hamifratz, I did not make the trip with them because Manya and Chaim put me under great pressure to remain with them.

One day Manya suddenly said to me, "We are leaving this place." "Going where?" I asked. "We are leaving, and you are staying. We are traveling to Israel, and we do not have the money to pay for your ticket." I was stunned. "But I brought you so much money," I shouted. "Where is all the money? And in addition, you didn't permit me go to the kibbutz," I added in tears. "You'll manage with the other Jews here," they said. When I saw them descending the stairs, suitcases in hand, my heart exploded with rage. They left, and I remained alone.

Once more I wandered around the city of Bytom without a purpose and without a home. At night I slept in the stairwells until one day I met up with a group of orphaned youths from Poland and Germany. There I met the wonderful group leader, Yaakov Rosenfeld, who was both a teacher and a father to us, a truly outstanding human being. He had known my family and was happy to see me. He convinced me to join them, to learn Hebrew and become a part of the youth group. "We must chart a new course for you," he said. Since the group in Bytom was small, we were joined several weeks later by another youth group. There I met another wonderful person, the group leader, Mottele (Mordechai Rozani).

In 1945, the year the war ended, we found ourselves in a kibbutz, a collective settlement, in the Polish city of Sosnowitz. We were a group of about eighty youths, boys and girls, all of us orphaned in the war, who had joined the youth movement, Hashomer Hatsa'ir, in order to reach Israel.

We studied Hebrew, Bible and General Studies. We learned Hebrew songs. The group leaders wanted, first and foremost, for us to regain our self-respect, confidence and joy in life, which the Nazi persecutors had robbed from us. To this end, psychologists and various professionals came to help us. The food at the kibbutz was meager, but the conditions we lived in were regarded as fine by orphans like us, used to hardships and suffering. And there were many positive things we enjoyed. We found comrades who had shared our suffering. Our mutual friendships helped us to recover and to open a new chapter in our lives. We loved the group leaders and our friends, and together we formed a close-knit and unified group.

Then anti-Semitism reared its head in Poland once again. One evening the Polish "bandits" threw rocks at us from windows. It was a miracle no one was seriously hurt. These were the same thugs who, but a short time before, had organized pogroms against the Jews of the city of Keltz, killing dozens of Jews there. Afterwards the Red Army arrived and imposed order in the city.

We considered various ways to leave Poland. This was not a simple thing to do. Every avenue of escape proved to be fraught with danger because the roads were still full of thugs looking to harm the groups of Jews on their way to Israel. We were frightened.

Our leader, Mottele, took us under his wing and promised the leadership of Hashomer Hatsa'ir that he would bring our group of orphans to Israel. He was quite fluent in German and other languages, and we began learning Hebrew from him as well.

From Sosnowitz we traveled by truck toward Bratislava to cross the Czech border. We were told to speak Hebrew if we were questioned, and to say that we were Jews from Salonika, Greece, who had been incarcerated in the concentration camps during the war. We were strongly warned that under no circumstance were we to admit that we were from Poland.

According to the plan, on the Czech side of the border representatives of the organization Habricha (The Escape) would be waiting for us. However, when we crossed the border there was no one waiting! We waited, meandering around, arousing suspicion. A local man asked what we were doing there. Apparently our answer did not satisfy his curiosity, for within a few minutes policemen of the Slovak gendarmerie arrived. After one glance at the mud on our boots, they whisked us off to prison, males and females separately. At night we heard talking on the other side of the wall. The conversation was in Polish. We called out and learned the "prisoners" were five youths of the Po'eyl Hamizrachi, who had also been caught as they attempted to cross the border from Poland to Slovakia. All night long we spoke together, exchanging tales of our experiences of escapes and imprisonments.

Several weeks later, J.O.I.N.T. obtained our release, and we resumed our trip. We reached a camp in Vienna, Austria. It was a transit camp for refugees, in the Baron Rothschild Hospital. There were hundreds of us, all Jews, waiting impatiently and in dire straits to continue on the long and arduous trip to Israel. Vienna had been partitioned among the four Allied powers, and the transit camp was located in the American sector.

We were housed in cramped quarters and slept in bunk beds. We received very little food, but we did not complain. We knew that much of Europe had been destroyed, that it was difficult to get food, and that the local residents shared our hunger as well. Even though we were presently confined—we could not go out and about freely in the city and the surrounding area—nevertheless, we lived with the feeling that the war was behind us, and fate had rescued us from death.

After a while we were transferred from Vienna to a transit camp in the small village of Salfelden on the Italian-Austrian border. It was another small step on the road to the land of Israel. We learned a bit of Hebrew there, as well as a great deal about the type of relationships that existed among the representatives of the various movements involved with the illegal emigration of European Jews to Israel.

Because of internal friction among the representatives of Beitar and Hashomer Hatsa'ir, we had to wait, and wait and wait some more. Arguments and even fist-fights broke out among the different representatives! Several times, the Beitar representatives attempted to start out on the journey, but representatives of other groups stopped them.

One winter day Mordechai Rozani and approximately sixty youths, males and females, who had undergone training at the Hashomer Hatsa'ir kibbutz, Hama'apil, were transferred to a training camp in Germany, in the village of Bernstein, near the Czech border. We settled into the large agricultural development, formerly owned by an S.S. officer who had been convicted of war crimes and sentenced to five years of imprisonment. We stayed there an entire year, learning a variety of agricultural skills; we grew vegetables and cared for the cows, chickens and geese. I became expert at milking cows and caring for the chickens, work that I especially enjoyed. The young men, Sioma, Emil, Isaac and others, cut clover, loaded sacks of grain and cleaned out the barn. We all went through a real pioneering program in preparation for our future in the land of Israel.

Near the clover fields, on the edge of the farm, lived a family of German peasants. There were many children in the family, and they eked out a living by doing odd jobs on neighboring farms, especially by doing work for a traveling circus that visited the surrounding villages. One day I went to pick wildflowers to decorate our dining hall, and I happened to meet the German couple. The wife invited me to visit their home. In the yard many children and chickens wandered about. The chickens drew my attention because of their unusual color. The German woman explained to me graciously about that particular strain of chickens and showed me one of them hovering over her eggs. Noticing my deep interest, she promised me that when the eggs hatched she would be sure to give me a pair of chicks.

One day the German woman came to visit our farm, a cardboard box in her arms. Inside was a pair of golden chicks with whom I fell in love instantly. I carefully tended them and became devoted to them, and the chicks quickly grew into a pair of handsome chickens, one male and one female. The male was a bit smaller than the hen, but his feathers were more colorful and brighter. Several months later the hen began to lay eggs, but suddenly both disappeared and could not be found anywhere. All my searching for them proved fruitless, and I sadly accepted the fact that, apparently, they had gotten lost or had been eaten by one of the dogs. Some weeks later I went to the forest with my friend Sioma to pick blackberries, and among the trees I heard a familiar clucking. We followed the sound and came upon an astonishing sight. In a single row marched the hen and fifteen small chicks. Bringing up the rear of the procession was the rooster. When they saw us they did not run away, but instead followed us all the way back to the farm.

We enjoyed every day we spent doing that agricultural work. We felt close to nature, to quiet and to the earth, but we were hoping for a "green light" from the representatives of The Escape so that we could set out on our way to Israel. From time to time representatives from Israel came to update us about what was taking place there. They told us about the British regime, about Tel Aviv and Jerusalem, and about the kibbutzim in Israel. From all their tales, as well as from other information, we managed to learn about what was going on in Israel. There were girls among us who were concerned most of all about having to shower in mixed facilities, men and women together. It is interesting that from all the stories of Israel this ridiculous misunderstanding seemed to have had the greatest impact upon us and seemed of the utmost importance.

One evening the leaders of our group told us to pack our belongings. "We are going to Israel!"

eight

To the Land of Israel

It was hard for me to leave the farm. It was especially difficult to part with the animals and the flowers. But emotions ran high, and we gathered up our belongings quickly. When the truck came for us we went wild with joy; we sang and danced. In my excitement I stumbled and fractured my leg. I sat in the truck, groaning with pain, but not for long. The knowledge that we were finally on the way to the land of Israel gave me strength and erased everything else from my heart.

But the joy was not complete. Someone was missing from the group; this was my childhood friend Sioma Gendelman, who was in the hospital after a tonsillectomy, and the German doctors adamantly refused to release him. Finally the group decided to smuggle him out. They helped him escape through a hospital window onto a canvas-covered truck, and from there we traveled straight to the train station to make the connection to the city of Marseilles, on the Mediterranean Sea in France.

In Marseilles we settled once again into a transit camp. It was a camp for Japanese prisoners of war, captured on the Pacific front, who were kept there, far from the battlefields. The buildings in the camp were made of hammered tin; we roasted in the summer heat and froze from cold in the winter nights. The camp authorities emptied several tin huts for our use, and we stayed there for a time, in conditions similar to those endured by the Japanese prisoners. With the meager amount of money in our possession we purchased coarse woolen blankets from the Japanese, and used them to sew warm slacks for ourselves, a scarce and precious commodity in chilly Europe.

After a while we were transferred to a new camp, run by Israeli representatives of the illegal immigration movement. We found ourselves in the picturesque village of Bandol, near Marseilles. We were approximately seven hundred women and men, old people and children. There were also pregnant women among us. We passed the time learning Hebrew and listening to lectures about Israel, playing a few games and engaging in sports, and sometimes merely doing nothing. My friend Bronya and I even enrolled in a crash course for kindergarten teachers, and we took care of over forty orphaned children.

The camp commander was a young man named Dan Ben-Amotz, an unusual character who eventually became famous as an artist and entertainer in bohemian Tel Aviv. He was fluent in Yiddish and Hebrew, and we learned Israeli songs from him and listened to exciting stories about the land and what was going on there.

Dan Ben-Amotz was always in a good mood. Very quickly he earned himself a reputation as a ladies' man. He was always surrounded by admiring females, and he changed partners frequently. A warm friendship developed between him and me. Bronya and I would request pencils, crayons and pictures of Israel from his office for the kindergarten we conducted. Sometimes we would have discussions. One time, he said to me, "You know, you are a beautiful girl" (*Du bist a sheyne meideleh*). He asked where I was from, whether I was from Poland or Rumania. I told him that I was from Poland, from a small village called Berezna, near the city of Rovna. Upon hearing my reply Dan became excited, and he said, "You know, I was born in Rovna," and he told me about emigrating to Israel with the youth movement before the war.

"Tell me, Genyaleh, do you wear a brassiere yet?" he asked me one time. "Will it make a difference to my future?" I responded. He quickly apologized for what he had said and complimented me on my beautiful legs. He was able to see my legs because I wore shorts sewn from old sugar sacks. Sometimes Dan was sharp-tongued and coarse.

It was the end of November 1947. We were completely cut off from what was happening elsewhere in the world. We had no radio, not even a newspaper. We didn't know that the United Nations was convening to decide the question of Israel's fate. On November 29, after the United Nations' vote, Dan Ben-Amotz assembled everyone for a celebration, and he broke the news about the United Nations' decision to establish a Jewish state in the land of Israel. We were overwhelmed by emotion. At this joyous moment Dan displayed his mean-spiritedness and lack of refinement. An elderly immigrant began to dance and to sing the "Hatikvah." Dan became angry at him and embarrassed him in front of everyone. He kicked him, pushed him and chased him from the group of revelers. He explained to us that when singing the national anthem one must stand at attention.

The guiding spirit of Bandol was embodied by Meir Hochberg, who joined the group after having spent the war years in Russia. He was older than we were and very intelligent, cultured and refined. He would produce plays with us, ask us to read books and then organize a mock trial of the book while serving as the judge. Hochberg was also the organizer and arranger of the *oneg Shabbat* (the "sweetness of Sabbath" parties), and I assisted him with this. In our Friday night performances we would frequently snipe at Dan Ben-Amotz because of his behavior. Even then we realized that Dan was not the right person for the job he was assigned to do. After we emigrated to Israel, my good friend Meir Hochberg joined the kibbutz Beit Kamah in the Negev. He died of a heart attack early in the 1990s.

Each and every morning Dan Ben-Amotz would conduct a roll call of all the people in the camp. When this daily line-up first started it created a feeling of unease; it seemed we were simulating the conditions endured by prisoners of war rather than those of refugees who had escaped slaughter. It was only natural that we would dislike these line-ups, accompanied as they were by all kinds of instructions for the day, and we found them very repugnant. In retrospect I would imagine that these line-ups were designed to meet the terms dictated by the French government to the camp organizers. It is important to remember that the French were hiding the illegal immigrants from the

English, giving us refuge and even pretending not to see us when we boarded the ships.

In December we set out for the ship that would take us to the land of Israel. It was a cold night. On foot we descended the narrow gorge that led from the camp to the seashore. We walked carefully in total silence to avoid detection. By the shore, rubber dinghies waited for us. Five people boarded each dinghy and immediately set out for the ship, which was anchored and waiting far from shore. Within minutes the dinghies filled up with water, and we became completely soaked. My woolen clothing absorbed the water and became heavy and cold. Shivering from the chill, we reached the ship and boarded, first the women and then the men.

It was a small, old ship that once had been used to transport wine, and its name was *The 29th of November*. In the storage hulk, wooden shelves had been constructed, two feet from one another, on which the casks of wine had been laid. Hundreds of freezing immigrants crowded aboard and huddled below deck on these cramped shelves, unable to move or even to lift their heads.

I will never forget how I boarded the ship. I was freezing and soaking wet and burning up with temperature. My woolen pants were so waterlogged and heavy that I could not lift my legs. Mottele Rozani, the leader, asked a few of the girls to take care of me, and they removed my wet clothing, changing them for some old underpants and slacks volunteered by one of the young men.

After several hours the ship set sail eastward. It was so cramped that in order to turn from side to side someone would have to issue a "command," and the entire row would turn in unison. Very soon all the passengers became seasick. The awful stench of vomit spread throughout the steerage. They would not allow us to go up on deck for fear that the British would notice our presence. We spent those days vomiting and trying to go on deck to inhale a bit of fresh air. I spent most of the trip lying on the plank, without eating, because I had no appetite. My friends urged me to at least drink some water. It was only after we reached Cyprus and showered in the communal showers that I realized how thin I had become during the trip.

The commander of the ship was a member of the Palmach, Mordechai (Moka) Limon, who later became a high officer in the navy. In Israel's history books he will be remembered as the officer who oversaw the "Ships of Cherbourg" campaign, when the transfer of ships built for the Israeli navy in the French port of Cherbourg was delayed because of the embargo France imposed upon Israel immediately after the Six Day War.

He was a tall and handsome fellow, who delighted everyone around him with his pleasant nature and cheerfulness. More than once I joined the group of girls who surrounded him. His warm personality helped us endure the hardships of the trip. I remember suffering a lot from nausea and vomiting. Moka would touch my shoulder and offer an encouraging word. His words worked miracles for me.

Near the Greek island of Crete we discovered we were being followed by a British warship, which escorted us to the port of Haifa. At times the British ship drew very near, and the soldiers aboard received a torrent of abuse and insults from our young men on deck.

After about twenty days, which seemed to us like an eternity, we reached the port of Haifa. Filthy and exhausted, thirsty and hungry, we disembarked and were immediately surrounded by British soldiers who tried to arrest us. Pandemonium broke out on the dock. We hurled canned food at them, packages of margarine and anything else that came to hand, but the solders did not retreat, and after feeding us, they loaded us on British warships to exile us to Cyprus.

Before they loaded us on the ships they sprayed us all with disinfectant to combat fleas and lice, and gave us water to drink and to wash with. After a day's journey we reached Famagusta in Cyprus. They herded us into a barbed-wire camp surrounded with watchtowers. We found ourselves living in tents under conditions we had become accustomed to in the camps in Europe. Here the conditions were actually better, for we had plenty of water and soap for washing. In the tent camp a cultural life started to flourish. We studied Hebrew, sang Israeli songs and were given lectures and guidance about life in Israel. On those days when there were no cultural or social activities we tended to laundry and food preparation. After three or four months the British released all the young people in the camp under the age of eighteen, myself among them. Once more we set sail for the port of Haifa. Preparing to disembark, we packed our few belongings. My personal bag contained a few books, two pant suits made from blankets and several pairs of slacks made from sugar and flour sacks. I also packed a faded dress that I had brought with me from Vienna.

We reached Haifa after the first cease-fire of the War of Independence. This time we came off the ship and were free to go. We prepared to go to the kibbutz, Yad-Mordechai, where the members of our group who had been spared detention in Cyprus had gone upon their arrival in Israel. On the way to Yad-Mordechai we stopped over in Tel Aviv. They put us up in the Sela Hotel on Hayarkon Street. The hotel was wretched, but we didn't care, for at least we had arrived in the land of Israel and had a roof over our heads. We didn't eat at the hotel but at an assembly hall just a few hundred yards away, on the road to Jaffa. These were warm and tasty meals prepared for us voluntarily by the women of Tel Aviv.

Jaffa was at that time an Arab city, in a state of constant warfare with the residents of nearby Tel Aviv. From the houses at the edge of the city snipers shot at passersby who came within the range of their rifles. However, after the long years of hunger we had endured during the war in Europe, we did not hesitate to endanger our lives by braving the Arab bullets in order to enjoy a hot meal. We would go to the hall under fire, ignoring the warnings of the local residents, "Be careful!" "Take cover!" We seemed not to know the meaning of fear.

Despite the tensions and battles, Tel Aviv in our eyes was like a magical place, an enchanting and exotic city. Even then it was the Jewish state's cultural center. We were delighted to discover theaters, movie houses and coffee shops. We loved the different types of food we had never seen before—ice cream, which we purchased for ten cents; yogurt, which I found wonderful; and the Arab pita bread. The beautiful stores and the well-dressed people made a strong impression upon us.

Heavy fighting was under way at that time in the south of the country, and we were not able to reach Yad-Mordechai. Some young people in our group did manage somehow to reach the kibbutz and were immediately drafted into the army; some were killed before they even understood why they were fighting.

The girls in the group and several of the young men were put up in the city of Rehovot. We lived in an inexpensive hotel and worked for the owner of a local orchard, picking citrus fruit, and with the paltry sum of money we received we managed to purchase food and other necessities. We loved working in the orchard. Every morning we would pack *lebeniya*, a handful of olives and a generous amount of bread and margarine. This is what comprised our daily fare. We would deposit the money we earned from working in a general fund, and we would make purchases as a group. Toward spring we were transferred, a few of us, to Kibbutz Hazorea. I celebrated my first Passover holiday in Israel on the kibbutz.

At Kibbutz Hazorea once again we lived in tents, four to a tent. Rooms indoors were solely for members of the kibbutz and not for us, the members of the illegal youth immigration. The kibbutzniks informed me that the bed I was sleeping in had belonged to a youth from Bulgaria who was killed in the War of Independence. All of his possessions were still in the tent, and I, sleeping in his bed, felt very upset.

They integrated us into the daily routine of work, in the kitchen, in the field and in the vineyard. I was happy that I was assigned to work in the kindergarten because they knew I had trained as a kindergarten teacher. In addition to the members of the kibbutz and the comrades of the youth immigration, there were also soldiers who had been wounded in the War of Independence who were sent there to recuperate. The soldiers received special privileges—delicacies such as chicken, coffee and cream were for them alone. Eliahu, who shared my tent, and I used to sneak a bit of cream to spread on a slice of bread, and it would dissolve to our pleasure. This was something worth celebrating compared to the inferior vegetables and filleted fish that were our daily fare. In the course of the afternoon containers of coffee and tea would be set up on the tables in the dining hall, with plates of bread, jam and fruit beside them. Open-mouthed with wonder, I would stand, gazing at the abundance of food and fruit.

One day my turn came for kitchen duty. The woman in charge was "Lenni, the Yekit" (German). My job included scrubbing the pots, peeling vegetables and helping out with anything and everything in the kitchen. When my week of duty ended Lenni realized that I truly knew how to cook. I told her about the period of time I had worked as a maid for a Ukrainian family, a period that had served me not only as a training ground for a possible career, but also as training for life itself.

One Friday afternoon Lenni told me that she was

going to the kindergarten to visit her son, who was ill. Two other female kibbutz members and I, who were on duty in the kitchen, decided to prepare a surprise for her. That evening, dinner included vegetable soup and an authentic meat goulash instead of the perpetual filleted fish, in addition to potatoes and rice. I seasoned the meat with spices and a bit of garlic and decided to cook the potatoes this time with their skins on, instead of serving the familiar mashed potatoes. Before serving, I sprinkled minced dill and black pepper on them. I also prepared the soup this time according to my liking, in the Russian style, with sauerkraut, bones, a bit of meat and potatoes. Lenni returned when everything was ready, and the Sabbath eve meal had begun.

The compliments rained down upon us immediately; some diners even applauded. Not one person wanted a substitute for the main course, and the majority stood in line for seconds. Everyone literally "licked their fingers." Lenni told everyone that "Zehava," from the Polish group, had prepared the food. This is what I was nicknamed in the kibbutz. From that day on my reputation as a superior chef was assured, and once again they refused to relieve me from kitchen duty.

Sometime later, they wanted to combine our group with a new kibbutz near Shadmot Deborah in the Jezreel Valley. It was suggested that I be sent to Kibbutz Merchaviah for special training in home economics to learn household sciences. I had no desire to turn cooking and kitchen work into my vocation. Memories of the difficult time I had spent in Maria and Petro's house were too fresh and too painful. I remained at Kibbutz Hazorea. I wanted to become a licensed kindergarten teacher, but my request for permission to receive formal training in this field was denied. Meanwhile my friends dispersed; the young men were drafted into the army, and the young women married and left the kibbutz. And we, the few who remained, were required to split Sabbath duty—milking, watering, caring for the sheep and so forth—among ourselves.

At the kibbutz we loved celebrating national holidays. The members always organized a dramatic performance. On my first Passover holiday in Israel at Kibbutz Hazorea, I was shocked. I remembered the Passover seder at the homes of Grandfather Noah Finkelstein and the rich uncle, Levi Nissingoltz. Here in the kibbutz we celebrated in a different style; even the atmosphere was totally different. The lengthy ritual of prayers recited in Grandfather Noah's home was dropped; in their place was singing and dancing. Everyone wore white, even we, the new immigrants.

The dramatic program, written by kibbutz members, included humorous parts, with piano playing and a chorus. They even made up the questions themselves. The "seder" was not celebrated ritually, as I remembered from my childhood so long ago, but was, in my eyes, more like a theatrical production, lacking any spiritual bond to our Jewish tradition. But it was an interesting experience, nevertheless. The food was very tasty, but I yearned for Mother's wonderful Passover dishes.

Afterwards we sang "Spring flowers will bloom, let's go and stroll in the field," and even if I did not understand all the words, I enjoyed the communal singing my friend

Elisheva lead. There was an atmosphere of joy and plenty of food, but I missed the personal warmth and love that had come to me at home. The kibbutzniks did not display much warmth toward us, the survivors, flaming brands rescued from the fire.

The loneliness was especially torturous during my free time. My friends would travel to visit relatives or acquaintances all over the country. They would spend their vacation time with their families, and I alone remained on the kibbutz. As a survivor of the furnaces of Europe, with a wounded and scarred soul, I anticipated and hoped for a warm and loving relationship with the members of the kibbutz. In this I was bitterly disappointed. The kibbutzniks never attempted to draw us close, to invite us to their homes. We always felt like we were on the outside looking in.

After a while my adoptive mother, Manya, and her husband arrived in Israel, and the couple settled in Rehovot. Once again Manya began to attempt to convince me to come live with them. This time I refused. I knew that I would be like a fish out of water outside the kibbutz. However, I would visit them on my holidays. I would hitchhike there because I lacked money for bus fare.

One time when I returned from Rehovot to the kibbutz after hitching a ride, I got off at the intersection known as the "Check Post," on the edge of Haifa. After a few steps I realized that two young men were following me. I did not know whether they were Jews or Arabs. They grabbed me and started pulling me toward a deserted field. I screamed and wept, but they persisted. Suddenly an idea flashed into my mind. "Leave me alone! I have tuberculosis!" I yelled in a hoarse voice. "I am contagious! I caught it in the camps, in the Holocaust!" After a brief consultation, they left me alone and ran away. I continued on my way, full of self-pity at having been forced to hitchhike. Nevertheless, I was pleased with my cleverness, which had led me to frighten off those youths successfully. My life experiences had made me into a fighter.

One day Berele, a young fellow I had known when I lived in the village of Berezna, who now lived in Kfar Yehoshua, came to visit me in the kibbutz. He told me that in Kiryat Chaim he had met someone who claimed to be a relative of mine, a man named Aaron Barder. I made contact with Barder, and he invited me to spend the Sabbath with his family.

I will never forget the warmth and homey atmosphere I felt in their home. They had no children, and his wife was a good and loving woman. Sabbath morning, a meal of radish salad with scallions and tomatoes awaited me, along with pickled herring, prepared just the way I liked it, the way Mother used to make it. After so many years of scrounging around and scrimping on food, I was served a Sabbath luncheon identical to the ones we had enjoyed in Father's home—gefilte fish and fragrant cholent, whose aroma filled the entire house. I treasured the memories of the tastes and aromas of that Sabbath for many years. Barder and his wife invited me to spend every holiday and vacation with them. And, indeed, I would visit them every fourth Sabbath, on my day off.

My tent-mate, Eliahu, was a well-mannered and kind-hearted young man. When it was his turn to clean, he would scrub the tent with his whole heart. Sometimes he even took my turn and cleaned instead of me. In exchange, I would wash his clothes for him. He had two shirts, and they were very precious to him. He had brought them with him from Europe. I would wash them by hand with love, and they were always in better shape than those washed in the main laundry.

We did not approve of the principle established by the youth movement, Hashomer Hatsa'ir, which mandated that males and females share living quarters. Nevertheless, we learned to live with the fact that we three girls and one guy had to share one tent; we even came to enjoy this arrangement. Eliahu and I loved one another like sister and brother. He worried about me and consulted me on everything, even romance. He, too, had known hardships and suffering, and the bond between us ran very deep. When I was ill with pneumonia in the infirmary tent, he was the only one who came during his breaks from work to bring me food. When any relative came to visit him, he would introduce me as "Genyaleh, my little sister."

Time passed, and Eliahu was drafted into the army. I sent him letters, and despite my lack of money, also managed to send him packages of nuts and sweets. Another tent-mate got married and left the kibbutz, and the tent emptied out. Once again I remained alone on the kibbutz, without family and friends. The time had come to effect a change in my life.

Despite all my reservations, I now decided to go to live once again with Aunt Manya, my adoptive mother. I was drawn to this decision by the pain of my loneliness, as well as by Manya and Chaim's persistence and their efforts to convince me to move in with them. I decided to leave kibbutz life and join them in Rehovot. I was delighted to find work immediately as a substitute kindergarten teacher, taking the place of a teacher who was on maternity leave. I was let go, however, when she returned to work several months later, and I found a job as a waitress in a coffee shop.

I was young and pretty with a curvaceous and full figure. A romance developed between me and one of the regular customers at the coffee shop. However, he subsequently informed me that since I had been through the Holocaust and medical experiments had been performed on me, I probably would not be able to give him children. Therefore he broke off all contact with me. I told him that I had not been in places where such experiments had been conducted. Nevertheless, because of his harsh words and painful attitude, I grew to dislike him and wanted nothing more to do with him.

Some time later the owner of the coffee shop told me that I was no longer needed, and once again I was left without the means of earning a living. Since I could no longer contribute money to Aunt Manya, I was ashamed to continue living with them and depending on them. I wanted some modern clothes, but I did not have a penny with which to buy any. Chaim was stingy, even though he had brought a lot of money with him from Poland. He would keep an accounting of each piece of bread I ate and each glass of milk I drank. Aunt Manya took pity on me and decided not to tell her husband that I had been let go.

Every morning I would leave the house as if on my

way to work, and I would spend the day searching for a new job. Finally I found one in the Workers' Kitchen. My job was to serve food and to scrub the giant pots. This was hard and exhausting work, and the pay was appallingly low. At the end of the work day I was so weak that I had no desire to go out and have a good time. I only wanted to sleep and sleep.

Those were days of scarcity and deprivation, and there was very little to eat. The day before the New Year, we received a gift from acquaintances who had a chicken coop: a hen without a crest, a bit lame but meaty, and thirty cracked eggs. In the neighborhood fish shop, we also purchased a big carp, and we brought all our precious items home, happily anticipating a holiday meal fit for royalty. While Manya and I went to finish up our shopping at the grocery, we appointed Uncle Chaim to keep an eye on the fish, swimming around in the bathtub, and the hen, which was laid out carefully on the marble countertop in the kitchen. When we returned we were horrified. A few bones were all that remained of the chicken, and only the tail of the carp was left in the bathtub. Our entire holiday meal had ended up in the belly of our neighbors' cat!

Aside from this incident, the days were routine.

One Friday evening I returned from work to Manya and Chaim's house. After the work day, I looked far from well-groomed. I was wearing khaki slacks and a blouse from the kibbutz, and my hair was a mess. A young man was sitting on a lounge chair on the porch, and Uncle Chaim introduced him to me. "This is Motti," he said. He told me that the man was the manager of a road-paving company that was currently working on a section of highway near Jerusalem. From what Chaim said, I understood that on his way from Jerusalem to the coastal plains, the motor of Motti's car had broken down. As it was near our home, Manya and Chaim had invited him to dinner.

The meal, that Sabbath eve, lasted longer than usual. Motti (Mordechai) spoke very little about himself. He told us that he had emigrated to Israel from Poland in 1938. His parents had sent him to Israel in order to study at the Hebrew University on Mount Scopus after he had completed his studies at the Hebrew Gymnasium in Bialystok. He had emigrated legally with several friends, with all the required documentation. His parents, two older sisters, Chaya and Devorah, and his younger brother, Moshe, had remained in the village of Zabludov, near Bialystok. They had all perished in the Holocaust at Auschwitz. After their death, Motti had changed his surname from Schwartz to Tuvi in honor of his mother, who had been named Tovah.

Despite his reluctance to discuss his own life, Motti showed a lively interest in mine. Before I had returned from work, Uncle Chaim had managed to tell Motti about the young woman who lived with him and his wife—a "daughter" who had lost her entire family in the Holocaust. Motti tried to learn as much about me as possible. At the end of the meal, Manya and I rose to clear the table, and Motti and Chaim, with the aid of a flashlight, went out to the yard to try to fix the car. Very soon they succeeded in revving up the motor. Motti went on his way, and Chaim came back to the house, a huge smile on his face. "Motti said that you are attractive," he said. "What do you think about him?" he asked, curiously. "I didn't pay much attention," I replied. "He looked okay," I said in an offhanded manner.

Motti and I began going out together in the evenings. We went to fine restaurants and enjoyed gourmet meals. We also went to see movies and plays. I remember going to Shakespeare's *A Midsummer Night's Dream* performed by the Habimah troupe. We enjoyed one another's company very much and shared the stories of our lives and our family histories. Motti spoke of his parents and of his brother and sisters, who had been killed. His father had been a well-to-do businessman who had owned a pharmacy in the village of Zabludov. His family was traditional but enlightened, the doors of the house open to intellectuals. His sisters had received higher education in the liberal spirit that characterized their home. Concerning himself, Motti said that he had served in the British Army's Jewish Brigade during the Second World War. He described the gory battles he had fought in as the British waged war against the Germans under the command of General Rommel in the Libyan Desert in North Africa. I told him everything that had happened to me, and he was shocked to learn of the tragic circumstances of my life.

This was the way our love story began. When Motti had finished work, we would go out to a restaurant and then later to a movie or play. One day Motti came and peeked through the window of The Workers' Kitchen to see me at work. He was shocked at the hard physical labor I was performing, and at my pale complexion. Relentlessly, he pressed me to leave that terrible job in the kitchen and promised he would find me easier work as a secretary in Tel Aviv. Sometimes we would sit on Manya and Chaim's porch, simply enjoying the peace and quiet of the town. Aunt Manya would peek through the shutters, supervising us like a policewoman. She and Uncle began talking about the beautiful wedding they would make me, with many guests and tons of food. But I answered, "What's the rush? I'm not getting married yet. We haven't even discussed it."

One day Motti suggested that we get married. I was eleven years younger than Motti, a nineteen-year-old who had known so much sorrow, and I saw no reason to rush. Motti did not pressure me, but he held out the promise of a warm and loving home, a secure financial future and a family. After four months of dating and one week pondering over what to do, I accepted his proposal.

When I told Aunt Manya about my decision to marry Motti, I hoped she would share my joy. But instead she said to me, "Why are you rushing? Aviva, my sister's daughter, is first in line. She is older than you and has to get married before you." Manya's family could not understand how little Genya, so small and skinny, had managed to hook such a wonderful bridegroom. Once again I was overcome by strong feelings of longing for my mother. I felt an urgent need to share my thoughts and feelings with someone truly close to me, a blood relative. I had been corresponding regularly with Grandfather Noah's sister, my maternal great-aunt, who lived in the United States. I felt that she would understand me.

Aunt Henya had arrived in America as a young girl and settled in the city of Baltimore. She had studied painting and ceramics and became a professional in those arts. She opened a large ceramic business. She found me after the war through the Red Cross. Aunt Henya loved me very much. After I wrote her, telling her about Motti, she sent her friends in Israel to check him out—what was he like, what was his background, was he (G-d forbid) already married, and other details she deemed essential. My wonderful aunt sent me a generous amount of money as a wedding present, as well as a beautiful trousseau that included sheets, towels and tablecloths, all of the finest cotton, and all of them monogrammed with the letter "G."

Motti was everything to me—father, brother, friend, husband and teacher. He was everything I had been robbed of so cruelly during the war. For the first time since my childhood had been lost, and since the deaths of all those I had held so dear, I had a real home, a true home, full of warmth and tenderness, just as Motti had promised.

Our financial situation was excellent. Motti was a skilled laborer and a hard worker. He had been a worker in a large construction company, and later he started his own small construction business. He was an outstanding family man, devoted to me and our two children, Vered and Tuvi. He was understanding and concerned, and he had the patience to appreciate my inner turmoil and spiritual agonies. Like me, he delighted in helping those less fortunate, and I continue until this very day in the path he paved.

However, fate did not allow even my happiness with Motti to last for long. One day, while pouring a concrete parapet for a multi-storied apartment house above the department store in Givatayim, he fell from the twelfth floor scaffolding and was killed.

This was in the month of March 1964. I was in my thirties, a young woman with the life experience of an ancient, full of hardships. At that point it seemed the door had finally slammed shut upon those old and painful memories. My suffering during the Holocaust was still very real, but now it faded into my past, for indeed I was now forced to struggle once more, this time with the difficult circumstances of life in the present.

Twenty years of tranquillity with Eli Zeltzer, my second husband, a sensitive mate whom I love, in a quiet neighborhood on the edge of Herzelia, have not erased the nightmares. A comfortable home, a yard full of flowers, a loving family; all these have not chased away the demons, nightmares that haunt dreams and phantoms that disturb my waking hours. I sought relief from my agony by reaching out to help the needy, as well as the new immigrants. Yet the memories have not vanished. Rather, they have become even more painful through the years. And now they are before you, in black on white.

Family Trees

Genya & Children & Grandchildren

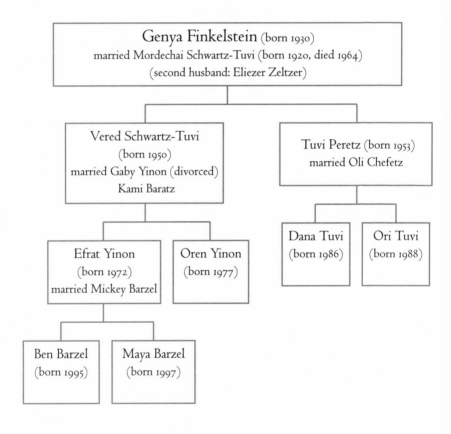

Genya Finkelstein (born 1930)
married Mordechai Schwartz-Tuvi (born 1920, died 1964)
(second husband: Eliezer Zeltzer)

Vered Schwartz-Tuvi
(born 1950)
married Gaby Yinon (divorced)
Kami Baratz

Tuvi Peretz (born 1953)
married Oli Chefetz

Efrat Yinon
(born 1972)
married Mickey Barzel

Oren Yinon
(born 1977)

Dana Tuvi
(born 1986)

Ori Tuvi
(born 1988)

Ben Barzel
(born 1995)

Maya Barzel
(born 1997)

Genya's Mother's Side

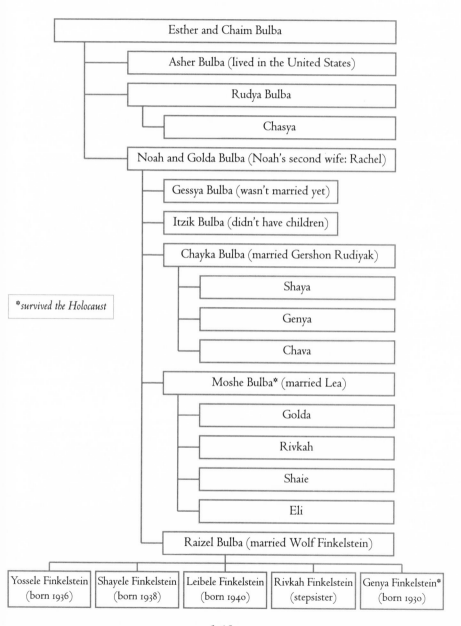

Esther and Chaim Bulba

Asher Bulba (lived in the United States)

Rudya Bulba

Chasya

Noah and Golda Bulba (Noah's second wife: Rachel)

Gessya Bulba (wasn't married yet)

Itzik Bulba (didn't have children)

Chayka Bulba (married Gershon Rudiyak)

Shaya

Genya

Chava

survived the Holocaust

Moshe Bulba* (married Lea)

Golda

Rivkah

Shaie

Eli

Raizel Bulba (married Wolf Finkelstein)

| Yossele Finkelstein (born 1936) | Shayele Finkelstein (born 1938) | Leibele Finkelstein (born 1940) | Rivkah Finkelstein (stepsister) | Genya Finkelstein* (born 1930) |

Genya's Father's Side

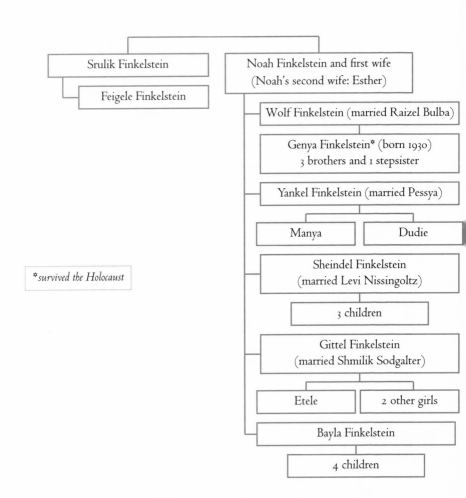

Srulik Finkelstein

Feigele Finkelstein

Noah Finkelstein and first wife
(Noah's second wife: Esther)

Wolf Finkelstein (married Raizel Bulba)

Genya Finkelstein* (born 1930)
3 brothers and 1 stepsister

Yankel Finkelstein (married Pessya)

Manya

Dudie

*survived the Holocaust

Sheindel Finkelstein
(married Levi Nissingoltz)

3 children

Gittel Finkelstein
(married Shmilik Sodgalter)

Etele

2 other girls

Bayla Finkelstein

4 children